T0198526

DO YOU KNOW
HIM?

A Collection of Stories and Poems about God, to God and from God

MARGARET WADSWORTH

WESTBOW
PRESS®
A DIVISION OF THOMAS NELSON
& ZONDERVAN

WestBow Press books may be ordered through booksellers or by contacting:

WestBow Press
A Division of Thomas Nelson & Zondervan
1663 Liberty Drive
Bloomington, IN 47403
www.westbowpress.com
1 (866) 928-1240

Cover photo is of the author's daughter, Sarah McDonnell, taken on the summit of Haleakala National Park by her 9 year old son Spencer McDonnell.

All Scripture quotations are taken from The Holy Bible, New International Version®, NIV® Copyright © 1973, 1978, 1984, 2011 by Biblica, Inc.® Used by permission. All rights reserved worldwide.

ISBN: 978-1-9736-6824-4 (sc)
ISBN: 978-1-9736-6826-8 (hc)
ISBN: 978-1-9736-6825-1 (e)

Library of Congress Control Number: 2019908934

Print information available on the last page.

WestBow Press rev. date: 9/23/2019

Dedicated to

My mom and dad

who bought me my first bound book
with blank pages, with the idea
that I would write a book someday.

Someday has come.

Acknowledgements

I had no idea there would be so many people I would go to for help in order to make writing this book a reality. I would like to thank David Church, who encouraged me to walk into the next season of my life. He was willing to read through my first draft and be ever so encouraging in spite of its rough edges. I would like to thank my editor, Dianne Steinley, who persevered in her work even with a broken arm and an extremely busy personal life. Also, many thanks to my friends Rachel Bertles, Donna Reid, and Lois Catlin, who gave me valuable feedback before I submitted the manuscript for publication. Then there was Susan Lee, who I didn't even know wrote poetry. She wrote a poem for me when I was overwhelmed and doubting my ability to complete this project. And best of all, my husband, Rick, who encouraged me all the way and kept saying, "I look forward to reading your book again."

Contents

Preface

I have always used poetry and writing as a tool to seek answers and to understand feelings that are so deep I can't express them verbally. As I write, I feel that God helps me put ideas together so I can understand them. I have also found that my love for Jesus has given me an unquenchable thirst for getting to know Him and hearing Him speak to me. I seem to hear Him best during the quiet time I spend with Him each morning. Sometimes I write poetry and sometimes I just write what I feel He wants me to.

I wasn't sure what to do with all my writing. I knew He would show me eventually. So, really, this book began many years ago.

One evening, I was supposed to be at a women's retreat at our church, but I was procrastinating. I stopped to make sure my daughter's babysitting job was going okay. I stayed until the baby went to sleep, even though it wasn't necessary and it meant being late to the meeting.

What I didn't know was that God was patiently waiting for me. When I arrived at the church, the little "get to know everyone" activity had just finished and they were starting to sing some worship songs. Nothing elaborate, just two ladies playing guitars, but I was swept unexpectedly into God's presence.

On this particular evening, God decided to answer my question about what to do with my writing. During the worship, He said, "I want you to write a book. Its title will be *Do You Know Him?*" I remember little else about that evening, except that now my writing had a bigger purpose.

That was a long time ago. Over the years I often became frustrated that I was too busy to write this book. I kept adding poems and reflections to the hard drive of my computer, but the time to put it all together never seemed to be right.

Upon our retirement, my husband and I received some advice on what to do in this next stage of our lives. We were given a vision of being in a field, a fenced pasture with a gate. My field was filled with flowers that stood for things I enjoy, like camping, skiing, golfing, playing pickleball, swimming, and so on. But there was a bit of a warning: the flowers I was picking in this field would die after a while. God wanted me to go through the gate and find *His* everlasting purpose in the next field.

That was fine, but I was really enjoying the flowers in the field I was in. I knew, though, that God would walk me through the gate when I was ready.

Then, we had a family tragedy. All those feelings from years before resurfaced and I knew I now needed to walk through the gate. It was time to share God's love with others in a way that He had planned so many years ago.

For Those Who Love Nature

As the sun creeps up following the night
And shines the creation of the day
So is it with the love of a friend
For they shine the creation of a smile

I have always loved nature: the beauty and quietness of a new snowfall, the artistic way colors are combined in the sky to open or close a day, or a misty rain.

I often wake up before dawn, but one morning I awoke just as the sun was making its appearance. I looked out my bedroom window, and the scene I saw turned into the following poem.

Sunrise

Streaks of blazing fire
Shooting from the eastern sky
Calling God's children

God's outstretched fingers
Cradling His creation
Opening the day

Memories are often heightened by our senses. The sense of smell is very powerful. It can be stored in the hidden places of our minds and resurface when we least expect it. This was the case as I jogged down the road and entered a new chapter of my life in British Columbia, Canada. When I married my husband, I moved from my home in Michigan to begin our life together here. The following is a memory inspired by a scent.

A Smell from the Past

As my feet find their familiar rhythm along the gently sloping road, I admire the valley where I plan to spend the rest of my life. The green hills are like mountains to me, and the ragged peaks off in the distance will be getting snow soon. The sun has begun its last blaze as it sinks behind the hill . . . I'd better run faster. My damp forehead tingles in the breeze as I round the mile mark. I run through a cool pocket of air, and there it is! That smell! Sweet, like roses, peonies and hyacinths all mixed together with a touch of spring rain.

I know it well, but from where? Ahhh, I remember . . .
    My mind
        drifts off
            into distant memories,
                memories that are as far away
                    as I am from my home . . .

Hiking to Twin Falls, in Glacier National Park, my family was like pioneers blazing the trail, each of us with our own carefully debarked walking stick. At age twelve, my heart raced with excitement as we headed into the trees that stood across the stream from our campsite. The snow-capped peaks stood solidly against the backdrop of the deep blue sky. The scent of the mountain air filled my entire being with awe as we witnessed the natural wonders that God had so meticulously sculptured for us to enjoy. Was it the air that smelled so sweet? Was it the trees? The flowers? Maybe the combined beauty of nature here in God's country? As we hiked on, the heat of the summer day filtered through the loosely woven greenery above. There was no need to use the dime-store canteens, for we drank straight out of the cool mountain stream.

I round the final curve toward my new home. The whole valley is in view as I see the beginnings of my new life before me. I realize a lifelong dream has been fulfilled by my Maker. Who else could have arranged the power of love to bring me to a place I had longed to live? That place is not within the shabby walls of our tiny rented farmhouse in a twenty-acre hayfield; rather, it's within the outstretched fingers of my Creator, opening up a new season of my life. A season of love, hope, and anticipation of a family and career shared with the man I love. Taking in a breath of the dusk-lit air, I walk down the long, narrow driveway. Thankful prayers, mixed with poetic images, threaten to erupt inside me as I walk into the house and scramble to find paper and pen. I sit down at our hand-me-down dining-room table and take one last look out the window. The sun has now gone, leaving me with only the memories of its descent.

Sunset in the Valley

The sun sets in the valley
Of a captured lifelong dream
I never thought I'd make it
Or never so it seemed
The sun is setting slowly
On the back side of the hill
But illuminates the mountains
Where the valley's lighted still

The sun sets further out of sight
And lightens up each peak
The moon comes looking for it
As if playing hide-and-seek
Highlights of light behind the clouds
Make colors in the sky
And bring a sort of peacefulness
You can't identify

The sky is getting darker now
The stars are coming out
To shine for those who watch them
As they're dancing all about
A mountain dream
Has now come true
Joined through the love
I've found with you

Coming out west from Michigan all alone was exciting. I was in love and I knew it was right. But it still was a huge change. I had to complete my teaching degree here and many of my credits didn't transfer. Even though the United States and Canada are very similar, there are hoops to hop through in addition to learning how to be an adult in a new place.

However, even with bumps in the road, I was always comforted by the beauty here. To this day, I still give thanks and can't believe I get to live here.

One of the summer courses I took was Environmental Education. On field trips we were asked to go out by ourselves and write. What an outlet for all the feelings that were bottled up inside me! It seemed more like a gift than an assignment for school. These next two poems were written as I sat in the trees on Knox Mountain in Kelowna, overlooking Okanagan Lake.

Going West

From the East I am coming, I am wandering out West
Where the frailness of my humanness meets the wilderness
I hear the birds, I feel the breeze
I see the hills all clothed in trees
A massive lake, so blue and long
As a life source flows along
Looking level with the land
Yet without water, canyon grand
The prettiest place I've ever seen
So much blue and so much green
Yet I feel out of place
Taken from my habitual space
A chance to make a brand-new start
A chance to have a change of heart
Lord, let me never take for granted
This wonderful place where I have landed

The Douglas Fir

At the edges of a clearing
I stand soaring toward the sky
My upper branches leaning
To escape the shade nearby
Lush green needles
Absorb the sunlight and the air
Towering well above
The other plant life everywhere
Dead, drooping bottom branches
Barely stay alive
Allowing for my canopy
To continuously thrive
My roots hold strong within the cushion
Of the compost forest floor
Absorbing all the richness
And keeping it in store
Resting in the shadows
Of the neighboring forest trees

I smell the warmth of pine tree air
As it dances in the breeze
Not blown easily by the wind
My branches barely stir
I am a year-long wonder
I am a Douglas fir

When our children were young, my husband and I bought a small cabin on Okanagan Lake. It was VERY rustic. There was an outhouse, no electricity, and we pumped our water at the sink. The beauty of this place was not where we slept, but where we lived out our summers outside. We were in a small bay, and every morning I would go out to the end of the dock before anybody else was stirring. The water was often like glass, and the Okanagan sun felt warm on my face. If anyone had seen me, they would have thought I was alone, but I was not.

Cabin Coffee

From deep within I hear Him speak
When everyone else is still asleep
The smell of coffee fills the air
Sounds of nature everywhere
Squirrels are running through the trees
A small breeze wafts
Through willow leaves
A woodpecker pecks upon a limb
I silently say a thank-you to Him
The water is so quiet and still
I ask Him to reveal His will
Out of the corner of my eye
A fish jumps up to snatch a fly
Minnows swiftly swim within
Blue-green water with sun-silvered fins
A small boat makes a ripple wake
Creating lines across the lake
The peaceful quiet begins to depart

For many now the day will start
But for me there's nothing greater
Than having coffee with my Creator

I was so in love with our little cabin spot and everything that it represented: the beauty of nature and the joy of family. I wanted to share that peaceful, wonderful feeling with everyone. Well, I almost did! We had a big extended family and our cabin was only twenty-five minutes from town. I was beginning to build a beautiful personal relationship with my Creator, and I wanted to share not only the cabin but my newfound relationship as well. I felt so blessed to have the summer space to share and enjoy. In one of my thankful moments, I wrote a small poem of gratitude.

Our outhouse was not your typical stinky box. This outhouse had two windows with yellow-and-white gingham curtains. The previous owner, an artist, had painted a mural on the inside showing multicultural children holding hands. When you sat there, you could see the cabin, the trees, and the lake in the background. It seemed like the perfect place to hang my poem.

Bless Our Little Cabin

Lord, bless our little cabin
And all who visit here
May we feel the peace
Of your presence being near
Let me take a moment
To meet you face to face
And thank you for providing
Such a beautiful place!

I enjoy all four seasons in Michigan and here in British Columbia. Winter means skiing and sledding and skating and playing in the snow.

Summer means camping and golfing and swimming and boating. Spring and fall are anticipation seasons that transition us from one to another. When spring and fall take longer than usual, I sometimes find it hard to be patient, and often my emotions follow suit.

Although it was spring, we still had a backyard full of snow. It felt as if spring would never come, and I couldn't quite shake the negativity I was feeling. To me, March means mud, and I felt as if my emotions were stuck in it! After I poured out my heart to God, I sensed He was telling me to go walk through my day and that He would be with me in the mud. He gave me the following poem.

Spring Mud

The winter seems long, and my mind is spending
Its time in dead thoughts that are never ending
I feel the frozenness melting away
With the promise that everything will be okay
And yet my spirit seems stuck in the mud
As I search for the signs of any spring bud
I know spring will come, and it always brings
So many new and beautiful things
As I listen to what You are telling me now
I am filled with new hope, but can't say just how
Maybe the clouds that bring us the rain
In my mind represent my perpetual pain
But then I see a small break in the cloud
And it's like I can hear Your voice calling out loud
"My rain is cleansing, and it brings new birth!
It washes away all the death from the earth
My Son will then come with His glorious light
And dry up the mud as He helps you fight
I know that you're finding it hard now to cope
Don't worry, My child, for I bring you hope
Just as spring rain comes before summer's sun
This battle you are facing is a battle I've won"

About six weeks later, we finally got back-to-back days with sunshine and warmth. For me, there seems to come a day when I feel that spring is finally here. That's when I become excited with the anticipation of summer. On this particular morning, I was so full of joy that I asked for a poem to illustrate what I was feeling. Right away, I knew it was a sequel to "Spring Mud."

Spring Sun

The mud of spring is drying up now
The clouds in my heart have left me somehow
The sky's opened up, showing beautiful blue
And the sun brings a joyful reflection of You
Spring flowers open with such vibrant color
And people seem happy to be with each other
Your joy seems to penetrate all of the earth
And nature gives praise with every new birth
May we shine Your light with unveiled faces
As we trade our clouds for the love that replaces
For God loves the earth and all who live in it
With the wind of the Spirit blowing within it
Son of God and Son of man
You've saved me from my mud again!

Even though we all go through physical and emotional seasons, The Father who made us promises to walk with us through them all.

For Those Who Serve

The Great Commission

Then Jesus came to them and said, "All authority in heaven and on earth has been given to me. Therefore go and make disciples of all nations, baptizing them in the name of the Father and of the Son and of the Holy Spirit, and teaching them to obey everything I have commanded you. And surely I am with you always, to the very end of the age. Matthew 28: 18-20

I believe we are all called to spread the word of God. The way we do it will be different for each of us. My job as a teacher prohibited me from saying many things. It's a good thing that God is not confined to the spoken word.

The Great Commission

Dear God,
You've asked us in the Great Commission
To go and spread Your word
As we hear You in our hearts
To speak of what we've heard
May You always keep on filling us
With loving things to say
To those who need Your comfort

As we live throughout each day
There's often not a footnote
Of a certain Bible verse
Or practiced words of dialogue
Remembered or rehearsed
But lead us each and every day
Through You to do our part
And speak the loving language
The language of Your heart

Years ago our pastor Ray and his wife, Mary Anne, not only decided to do missionary work in Burundi, Africa, but actually moved there. Yes, sold their house, packed up, and relocated there. Our church is known as a church that equips and sends people off to spread the word of God. Yet it still amazes me to see people with faith unshakeable enough to put God first, even before children and grandchildren.

Matthew 10:37–38 says, "Anyone who loves his father or mother more than me is not worthy of me; anyone who loves his son or daughter more than me is not worthy of me, and anyone who does not take his cross and follow me is not worthy of me."

That doesn't mean we are all called to leave our families to go to other countries. It does mean that we need to make God first in our lives and follow Him, wherever He tells us to go. For me, it would be almost impossible to leave my family. And yet some of us are called to do just that.

At one point, Ray and Mary Anne's daughter was able to visit them for the first time. I was very excited for her, since I had put myself in her shoes many times with thoughts like, "But Mom and Dad, I know God is calling you to do this, but I'm having a baby!"

Burundi has been extremely blessed by this couple, and much rejoicing goes on in our church and community when we hear of the great things God has accomplished because of their faithfulness.

Before Ray and Mary Anne left, our church got together to pray for them. They had pastored our church for many years and had led us into our own building for the first time. This move was a huge change, not only for them, but for the church body. During that service, I received this poem:

Your Mission

As you leave to do your part
Go reveal the Father's heart
It's obvious that your hearts have heard
Just how to act upon God's word
Though you may not understand
What His will is through your hand
Your weakness He will use to do
The work that you allow Him to
We thank you for the bricks you laid
When our foundation first was made
God has for you another mission
To carry out the Great Commission
Go with our prayers and blessings too
For God's anointing is on you
So spread your wings, be free to fly
Know the Father is nearby
May you know just what your part is
And how to share where Jesus' heart is

Ray's birthday is in the same month as mine. My daughter's gift to me was making a special dinner for her dad and me. On the forty-minute drive home, I thought about Ray being halfway around the world and not being able to spend his birthday with his family. I prayed that he would always have peace and continue to share God's love with all those orphans he was caring for. My prayer ended up in the following poem.

May You Always Have SONshine

May you always have SONshine
Your anointing increase
May you always have vision
And a heart filled with peace

May you feel His mercy
Be blessed by His grace
May His love overflow
And be seen in your face

May you always have purpose
Discernment galore
May you always be sharing
His love evermore!

Being part of a small church has many benefits. Not only can you publicly announce birthdays, but when people in your congregation are going through times of sadness or experiencing a joyous occasion, the whole church body experiences it as well. When Ray and Mary Anne left, our friends Clint and Sharon began pastoring our church. Watching God's call on their lives from such a short distance made me grow tremendously and learn more about the blood, sweat, and tears that go on behind the scenes. I appreciated the work Ray and Mary Anne had done even more, as I watched our friends fill their shoes. I asked God to give me a poem to bless Clint and Sharon.

Those Who Serve

May You grow them and guide them
Be fruitful inside them
Help them lead others Your way
For in all that they do

May it all be for You
As they love You and serve You today

At this point, we had two pastors, even though one was pastoring far away. Communication between here and Africa can be sketchy at best, but we kept close as well as we could.

Apparently, Burundi can get foggy. I can't remember why this was a problem, but our church was asked to pray. Ray and Mary Anne were on my daily prayer list and I always welcomed specific things to pray about. The following is what was given to me to pray for them.

Morning Mist

May God give a morning mist
As you start your day
A calm, refreshing coolness
That comforts you, I pray
For some this morning mist
Will bring about defeat
But God's people have His word
As light upon their feet
May you be in the place today
Where He needs you most
And fill your hearts with praise
Among His heavenly host
Let Him direct your hands
And help you to persist
For what is fog to others
Is to you a morning mist

With all the life-and-death stories of miracles we heard, these seemingly smaller miracles speak to me even more because I can relate to them on such a personal level.

About a year after the last poem I wrote for Ray and Mary Anne, they became the proud adoptive parents of a little two-year-old African boy who had been orphaned by the Gatumba massacre in 2004. Again, I was amazed at how strong God's anointing was. He had shown me time and again that if He calls us to do something, He will give us the strength to do it. You must understand that Ray and Mary Anne are grandparents many times over. They had faith that God would continue to provide the energy needed to not only raise a toddler but help pastor a church of thousands, be the headmaster of a school, and help oversee the homes built for so many orphans. Their faith again strengthened my faith. Hence, another poem.

Bless You

Bless you in the busyness that people cannot see
Bless you for the work you do, on behalf of Thee
Bless you for being parents the second time around
Bless you as you take a stand on heaven's battle ground
Bless you as you pray for those in greatest need
May you be blessed as you are called
To parent, teach, and lead
Know that you are thought of, prayed for, and held dear
When serving God in Africa just as you did here

Lorraine, my neighbor and friend, was moving. She and her husband had talked about it for years. Finally, the time was right, and it was actually happening. Even though she lived only two doors away, we had lost touch a bit now that our kids had grown up. But this dear friend was the one who God had assigned to help me know Him personally. My parents had done a wonderful job teaching me *about* God; but as in growing up in every other way, we need to stand on our own and know God personally for ourselves. When I had sensed that something was missing in my life, God had put Lorraine in my path.

Now, after what seemed like a lifetime, she and her husband sold their house, bought a fifth-wheel trailer, and were retiring for a year of helping others.

I couldn't believe the time had gone by so fast! This was the last Sunday they would be in church, and I was ashamed that I hadn't done something special for her yet! People were praying for them, and I wanted to let Lorraine know how special her friendship had been. God was merciful and answered my cry for a poem.

Bless My Friend

Lord, bless my friend as she moves on
For she is one I depended on
A strength to others as to me
As she fulfills who You want her to be
I know in life there are many changes
Your purpose for us rearranges
I thank You, Lord, for it was through
Lorraine that I was drawn to You
Please keep setting people free
Through her the way You did for me

There was a time where I seemed to receive poems for specific people. Some of them I knew well, but some were in my path for only a short time. Summer was in the latter group. First I loved her because I loved her name. She was very soft-spoken and had a peace about her that I admired. She and her sister once spoke at our church, and their message left an imprint on my heart.

Ironically, my new friend Summer was negatively affected by the low valley cloud that is common here during our winters. Even though I love Okanagan winters, this poem has also helped me whenever I've been unable to see the sun (or the SON) in my own situation.

Summer's Sun

In all of My glory
I'm shining on you
When the sun doesn't shine
I'm still shining on you

When I become silent
With clouds heavy upon you
My radiant presence
Still reflects on you

Just like the sun
Does not change in the sky
I am unchanging
And I hear your cry

Depend on My strength
And seek always My face
For it shines like the sun
And communicates grace

How do you do this?
You've asked for direction
Dear Summer, just look
Where I leave my reflection

As I mentioned earlier, when our friends Clint and Sharon took on leadership of our church after our previous pastor and wife went to Africa, it was a real eye-opener. Being a responsible parent is one thing, but being spiritually responsible and the go-to person for a large group of people is quite another. My husband and I really felt that being supportive friends was even more important now, so they were often in my prayers.

Prayer for Pastor and Wife

Lord, may You bless them and keep them, I pray
Support what You will do through them today
Give them a balance of family and work
Provide them with a supportive network
That will pray through the trials and give them advice
Remind them that Your grace will always suffice
May they hear Your will for our congregation
And protect their children from evil's temptation
Please keep them healthy, humble and fit
Filled with the joy from the Holy Spirit
In You may they find repentance and rest
Love, peace, and joy and divine happiness

Our friends need our prayers in all situations. Just because you love God or you are leading a church doesn't mean you are protected from the everyday aches and pains of life. Ephesians 6:18 says, "And pray in the Spirit on all occasions with all kinds of prayers and requests. With this in mind, be alert and always keep on praying for all the saints." So I did this when Sharon had a painful abscessed tooth.

We Lift Our Friend

Lord, give our friend Your comfort and peace
Please let Your Spirit be released
For as she walks within Your light
May she be pleasing in Your sight
May she reflect Your love and grace
As You heal her in this place
Carry her with arms of joy
May Your presence she enjoy
As she lifts this day to You
We lift our friend up to You too

Clint had suffered with terrible back issues for a long time. He was in tremendous pain every day. It was fantastic to hear that he was finally going to get the surgery he needed. We gathered at the church to pray for him the night before. The next morning was a school day and during my quiet time I prayed for him and received a poem. I don't know where I found the time, but I typed it up, framed it, and took it to the hospital, all before going to school to teach. I had to leave it with the nurses on the surgery floor because he was already being prepped for surgery, but he got it and I think he was even able to read it before he went under the anesthetic. Talk about perfect timing!

The Great Physician

Lord, please bless my friend today
And shower him with grace
Give him ears to hear Your voice
And eyes to see Your face
Help him taste the sweetness
And the power of Your word
May he feel Your presence
And help him rest assured
That he's got the Great Physician
Doing surgery today
May Your healing touch increase
As Your people pray
For You are the healer
Of the body, mind, and soul
You have amazing power
To make a person whole
So I lift him up to You
Place him in Your loving care
I can feel at peace
For I know that You are there

We are all accountable for our actions, but the people who teach about God and guide others have a great responsibility to hear from God clearly and do His will, not their own. This life career is a huge undertaking that requires lots of prayer and support from family and friends. So I wrote a poem especially for Clint and Sharon's twenty-fifth wedding anniversary:

Marriage Career

Twenty-five years ago
A couple pledged as one
And God knew from the start
Something special had begun
For His plan was perfect and
His timing was unique
And He trained the two of them
To listen to Him speak
Now they don't just listen
But they act on what they hear
And they have made the love of God
Their marriage and career

In the time we have been going to our church, we have had four different pastors. Different leadership brings different flavors, depending on the personal philosophy and personality of the one leading. We all have different gifts, and our church family, as a group, is always changing. It was during one of these changing times that we were getting a new pastor. As we were inducting him and his wife during the worship part of the service, I got an interesting vision that was completely unexpected.

I saw many beads lying out on a surface, all disconnected. These beads represented our fellowship. They reminded me of the beads I often let my students use to make necklaces. But I was quickly corrected as I felt God say, "No, these aren't beads; they are all beautiful jewels! And this new pastor and his wife are here to connect them together."

His Precious Jewels

Vernon Christian Fellowship
With many precious jewels
Laid out on the workbench
Of the Mighty One who rules
All shining in their special way
But somehow disconnected
Yearning for community
Our Trinity reflected
God has sent an answer
To our congregation's prayer
Someone to connect the jewels
Within God's loving care
To edify the Father
And give glory to the Son
Living by His Spirit
Uniting us as one

Because our church was going through a time of change and unrest, I was reminded of something God had inspired in me years before. How precious are the gifts God has given us to grow and share with others for His glory. And what a wonderful blessing it is when we can see past the faults of others and glean from the gifts God has given them.

When I received this, it was a personal word for personal circumstances, but I can now see that it applies corporately as well.

$\mathcal{F}or\ \mathcal{T}hose\ \mathcal{W}ho$
$Celebrate$

We experience many significant events in our lifetimes, such as births, weddings, holidays. Many of them make us reflect in such a way that we feel the need and excitement to celebrate with others. Often, they are times when we know, somewhere deep inside, that we are part of a plan that is bigger than ourselves.

When I gave birth to my children, I felt a love beyond words. Somehow, I knew that this love had something to do with God. Thinking back, I would say that maybe that was the beginning of my search to find the meaning of life and the source of this unexplainable love. I wrote this poem to explain what I was feeling.

The Joy of Motherhood

Nine months of anxious waiting
And long-term preparation
For the task of motherhood
A cherished occupation
You carry them around with you
They go wherever you go
And you can feel them inside
As they mature and grow

And when you meet your son or daughter
See them face to face
There's a feeling that you can't explain
And no one could replace
No introductions necessary
You've known them all along
Since those soft kicks inside you
Until their crying song
You snuggle with them gently
And hold them to your breast
It was hard work for both of you
And now it's time for rest
Such a tiny little person
So tender and serene
They're hardly ever dirty
And they always smell so clean
Part of Mom and part of Dad
And no one can compare
The excitement and the love
And the joy new parents share!

Once I knew more about this incredible kind of love and I had discovered and experienced the source of it, I wanted to include it in everything. It wasn't religion I had found but a relationship. One that was deeper than the love I felt for my babies; one that was even more exciting than my first love, or the committed love in my marriage. I found it ironic that this overwhelming experience I wanted so much to share with people was one that people could only appreciate if they, too, were searching for it. And if they weren't, you could easily offend them. I knew that first hand because I had been offended that way myself.

At the same time, I wanted people to see this new love in me, so I had to do something. I wanted people to think about the possibility that God has a perfect design for marriage and it is supposed to last forever. (But you will probably need His help.) And so it started showing up in my writing. Since my husband and I both felt that our meeting was orchestrated by God (even though we weren't very close to Him during our first years together), I wanted to somehow write about it without sounding churchy or religious. These two poems were given as gifts. The first one was framed, and the second accompanied a wreath for the front door.

Marriage

Marriage is a covenant
That's like a living vine
Growing stronger
And more beautiful
As two lives intertwine

Marriage is a living vine
Winding through the years
Loving, caring, hoping, sharing
Laughter, life, and tears

Marriage is a family vine
According to God's plan
Learning, living, and forgiving
Since the world began

The Wedding Wreath

The wedding is over
The papers are signed
Both bride and groom
Have been wined and dined
A honeymoon filled
With travel and fun
To celebrate two of you
Officially one
A small, lovely wreath
To hang on your door
To remind you that love

Is for evermore
For just as a wreath
Circles round with no end
I pray that your love lasts forever . . . Amen!

I always enjoy writing little poems inside homemade birthday cards. These are personal to the person I write them for, so of course they are not included here. But because I just wrote about marriage, I thought I would include one birthday poem I wrote for my husband, Rick.

Growing Old Together

You are the one God chose for me
I've always known it's true
That there is no one anywhere
Who fits with me like you
So I plan on celebrating
November tenth forever
And we can feel blessed that we
Are growing old together!

My mom was a quilter. If you know one quilter, you probably know three. Quilters attract one another like small children attract one another. My mom became involved in a group called Prayers and Squares in her church. They would get together and make lap quilts and visit. If someone you knew was sick or perhaps dying, you could request such a quilt from their group. But what you got was so much more than material squares sewn together. Little strings held all the squares to the backing. Anyone wanting to pray for the sick person would say a silent prayer as they tied these strings. The quilt then went to the person with love and prayers to aid in their healing.

When my mother-in-law got sick with pancreatic cancer, I asked my mom to send me a quilt for her. At that time, my mom lived in Michigan and I lived in British Columbia, Canada, so my request could by no means happen overnight. I'm sure the prayers made it on time, even though the quilt arrived as we were planning her memorial. I keep the quilt as a reminder that our love and compassion for one another are important and powerful. That being said, our prayers are not like coins inserted into a miracle machine. We need to believe our Heavenly Father knows what's best in the bigger picture and we may never understand His decision in this life. Our requests may still be answered with a loving "Not this time," as mine were. Here is a poem about the quilts made with so much love, often for people these quilters didn't even know.

Quilt of Love

This quilt was made of love and caring
For you because we felt like sharing
The thing that makes life all worthwhile
Love

With every stitch, from every hand
Every square uniquely planned
Reflecting what's behind your smile
Love

Pinning every piece just so
The quilt began to grow and grow
To illustrate your special style
Love

Pressing in each little piece
Anticipation did increase
For we would share in just a while
Love

And when it all was sewn together
It represented what's forever
Woven into all the squares
Our thoughts, our hopes
Our dreams, our prayers
Of Love

One day, I was ironing and mentally planning for Thanksgiving. We have a large family on my husband's side and at that time the holiday dinners were often at our house. I took Thanksgiving seriously because I was so thankful for so many things, especially the changes in myself. Even though many of our family members didn't say grace at every meal, they knew we did, so I prayed for a prayer of Thanksgiving to share. I wrote as I ironed and the following was used as the blessing before we ate that Thanksgiving:

Thanksgiving Prayer

Almighty God in heaven
We thank You for this day
We thank You for Your Son
And the price He had to pay
He didn't go get even
Or complain it wasn't fair
He simply said, "Forgive them"
As they hung Him there
No amount of jewels
Crops or livestock would suffice
It took the perfect man
To make the sacrifice
You asked us to remember You
Each time that we break bread
So together we recall You carried
All our sins upon Your head
Lord, thank You for this family
For You knew us from the start

And I know we hold a special place
Deep within Your heart
Be with us through all our trials
Help us to see Your way
Jesus, I'm so thankful for You
Each and every day

My husband must have really liked the poem. One day I got a phone call from him during my lunch break at school. He started playing his guitar and surprised me by singing my poem! It has always been part of the many songs he sings, and, whenever I hear it, I am swept back to the afternoon prayer I prayed as I ironed.

Easter is my favorite holiday because it has a little less fluff and stuff to distract us from its real meaning. Yes, Christmas is about *when* Christ was born, but Easter is about *why* Christ was born. Christmas is so over-commercialized. We can spend more than a month preparing for it and the meaning gets lost.

But Easter is so special that Jesus told us to remember it all year long. One Easter morning, I was feeling very excited because all my grown kids and their spouses were coming to church for the Easter service. I wondered how many other people had invited their families to come and, if this was not a weekly occurrence, what was their reason for coming? Whatever it was, I wanted them to feel welcome. So God gave me this poem that morning before we left.

Why Did You Come?

Maybe you came today
To worship Christ the King
Because He died and rose again
He gave His everything

Maybe you came today

To search inside your heart
Because you knew God once
But that somehow fell apart

Maybe you came today
Because you feel lost
You've thought about a life with God
But felt there'd be a cost

Maybe you came today
Out of respect or obligation
And you feel you're not ready
To accept God's invitation

Whatever brought you here today
We hope that you'll pursue
A relationship with the LIVING God
Because He's so in love with you!

HAPPY EASTER!

One weeknight, I watched a movie that I did not really have time to watch. Being a teacher, I always had homework to mark in the evenings, so trying to make time on a weeknight for something extra was a real stretch. But we had a movie night at our church, and my husband and I thought we should go. I went, but halfheartedly. In fact, I brought my marking to do while I watched it, sitting at the back so I wouldn't offend anyone. But the message was so good, I never opened my backpack. It was around Eastertime. Not only did I take the time to watch the movie, but it inspired me to write what turned out to be an Easter message.

Perfect Love

Similar to the parables of old
The teaching stories that our Savior told

Were based on topics so well known
And listeners made them all their own
The story of God's love for you
It is timeless like those stories too
When I was a child there were some things I knew
Love meant having a mom and dad too
Moms and dads were to come as a pair
And happiness was supposed to be there
Was this the perfect love I strived for?
Or maybe there was something more?
When I grew older and I fell in love
With the person chosen by God above
I knew this was to last forever
And that I should stay with this person forever
This love seemed so much bigger than me
And deeper than I thought it could be
Was this the perfect love I strived for?
Or maybe there was something more?
Now there were struggles along the way
But deep in my heart I knew I should stay
Then I gave birth and each time was the same
For there was a deep, different love that came
A lot less selfish, and forgiving this time
And I started to think about love one more time
Was this the perfect love I strived for?
Or maybe there was something more?
Again there were struggles along the way
And I needed to pray just to get through the day
And then as a grandma, oh my, could there be
A more fulfilling love that was free?
And I thought about how my heart had grown
And the strength I now had that wasn't my own
For my love isn't perfect, how often I fail
Compared to God's love, mine's so low on the scale
When my friends let me down, when my kids disobeyed
I'm not very nice when I feel I'm betrayed
And then I got thinking, isn't it odd
How often I do this same thing to God?
Selfishness, anger, and impatience exist

And all of these things are so hard to resist
I reject what He teaches, I pretend I don't care
I go it alone and pretend He's not there
Because the love that we carry within
Will never be perfect because of our sin
We needed a Savior, so He gave us His Son
Because He knew what had to be done
God sacrificed His only Son
And on Easter declared the victory won
He loves you so much and hopes you'll believe
So you'll open your heart and make space to receive
This perfect love that He has for you
For then you'll get better at this loving thing too

Good Friday and Easter Sunday are a demonstration of this love. Jesus explains love in John 15:13: "Greater love has no one than this, to lay down one's life for one's friends."

For Those Who Suffer

Isn't it interesting that
we have so much trouble having faith
in a God that we cannot understand.
And yet,
in our times of great need
we call on the power of the God
who is beyond our understanding.

I warn you. Parts of this chapter are sad. You may not want to read it in one sitting, as I did not write it in one sitting and the events took place over many years. What I hope you will come to realize, though, is that during the saddest and hardest times of our lives, God is there. And He is loving us even more than we can ever imagine. I believe it is in these times that He speaks a bit louder because He wants so much for us to hear Him and feel His comfort.

During one such time, my husband and I were dealing with a real scare. During a routine physical, he complained of losing his breath once in a while, so he was tested for asthma. When it was not that, they did further testing and found a mass in his chest.

Yes, it was cancer, and yes, it was treated, and yes, he was eventually fine.

But, as you can imagine, this took months of testing, surgery, and radiation treatments. The scariest part was the not-knowing time. The guessing time. The "what if?" time. These are the times I try to rely on the power of God that is beyond my understanding. And I felt God's comfort as I wrote this poem:

Pockets of Time

There are pockets of time
Filled with too many tears
Remembering you and me
through the years
There are pockets that hold
The planning that's needed
In case life on earth
Is abruptly defeated
There are pockets of tenderness
Soft conversation
Moments of thankful appreciation
There are moments of dreams
To quickly fulfill
Listening for
The voice of God's will
There are pockets
BIG pockets
Of time spent in prayer
As He reminds us
He'll always be there
We can have peace
For God has a way
Of giving us just
What we need today
So together with God
Today we will stand
For tomorrow is left
In His capable hand

I was beginning to realize that prayer was not just saying memorized words that rose like incense up to heaven. I was writing poems that were prayers to express my thoughts and feelings. I had always written for this purpose, but now, with a personal relationship with Christ, I felt that somehow God spoke to me through what I wrote. He gave me hope as I put words to paper; something I found difficult to do in conversation. I used to think I was "writing" poems, but as I look back and remember, I realize these poems were actually prayers. Amazingly, it is as if God helped me pray/write them so He could comfort me through them.

One of my new friends from the church I was attending was diagnosed with breast cancer. She was one of the first people I knew personally to have cancer. It was terrifying because the few people I had known to have the "C" word had died.

This was one of the first prayer poems I wrote for our friend, who, thankfully, is still with us today.

Give Us Faith

Lord, give us Your peace throughout this trial
We ask for Your comfort and grace for a while
Because, Lord, we are troubled and we don't understand
All the reasons behind Your sovereign plan
Please give us the faith Your Spirit provides
Especially now when we're hurting inside
In everything may we seek Your face
Because it is there we will find Your grace
We know in You all things are okay
For You'll give us the strength that we need today

When I moved to British Columbia from Michigan, where I had grown up, I knew it was right as sure as I knew my own name. I was in love and planning to marry the person I felt God had chosen for me, even though I didn't have a personal relationship with God at the time.

Maybe that is why it wasn't hard to leave my family and friends in Michigan. Looking back, I can't even believe I had the guts to do it. If I had calculated not being able to attend all the weddings, or say final good-byes to loved ones, or be as involved in other events with family and friends, I may never have had the courage to make such a giant move.

I felt devastated when I received a call at school from my brother, telling me that our mother had breast cancer. I cannot begin to explain the helplessness I felt. Even with three young children and a teaching job, I wanted to jump on a plane right that minute. My brother convinced me that I should stay home and we would keep in close contact. So I did what I could do from miles away. I prayed.

Be with My Mom and Dad

Dear Lord
Be with my mom and dad today
Please keep them in Your care
It breaks my heart I must be here
And not be with them there
I thank You for the strength You give
And I really do believe
Your blessings over all the miles
Are there to be received
It's when I keep my eyes on You
I feel the greatest peace
And know that Your great love for us
Just waits to be released
For when we bring our cares to You
When life appears unfair
Your comfort is consoling
When I go to You in prayer
I know that You are with her
Every step along the way
May Your Spirit keep us close
As I struggle through today

My mom came through the surgery and treatment with flying colors. Even though I bought her the coolest hat ever, she didn't even lose her hair!

God had answered the prayers for my friend, my mom, and my husband just as He answered Hezekiah's prayer many years ago:

> In those days Hezekiah became ill and was at the point of death. The prophet Isaiah son of Amoz went to him and said, "This is what the LORD says: Put your house in order, because you are going to die; you will not recover." Hezekiah turned his face to the wall and prayed to the LORD, "Remember, O LORD, how I have walked before you faithfully and with wholehearted devotion and have done what is good in your eyes." And Hezekiah wept bitterly. Before Isaiah had left the middle court, the word of the LORD came to him: "Go back and tell Hezekiah, the leader of my people, 'This is what the LORD, the God of your father David, says: I have heard your prayer and seen your tears; I will heal you. On the third day from now you will go up to the temple of the LORD. I will add fifteen years to your life. 2 Kings 20:1–6

It is wonderful when God answers our prayers the way we hope He will. We are full of faith and joy and hope for the next tragedy that may come our way. But what happens when we don't get what we ask for? How do we feel when the person dies even when we pray, when we get others to pray, when we cry ourselves to sleep?

During my teaching career I had this happen. There was a wonderful little girl in my class with cystic fibrosis. She had regular doctor appointments at the children's hospital about six hours away from where we live. After one of these appointments, I received a call to tell me she was not doing well. I cried, I prayed, and I pleaded. In my pain, I wrote.

I Know

You know what's best for Maddy
I don't have to understand
For I know You hold Your children
Safe within Your hand
I know You understand the pain
We all are going through
For many, many years ago
Your only Son died too
You showed us that Your love for us
Was worth a father's pain
And then You raised Him from the dead
To show there's life again
And so I know that Maddy's safe
Although I don't know why
I also know that healing
Happens even as I cry
I know that You're the Comforter
Through every living chapter
As we travel through the book of life
Until life ever after

That poem was helpful for me as I spent my weekend crying and praying. Yet in the end, Maddy did not return to our class. I was grateful that I was given private time to try and process this. But how was I going to explain to a class of seven-year-olds that their friend was not coming home from her doctor appointment? The counselor at our school referred me to the book *Lifetimes: A Beautiful Way to Explain Death to Children* by Bryan Mellonie. I was so thankful that she was able to be there with me as I read it.

I don't remember the exact words I used to break the news to my students. But the book was so wonderful that it was also a comfort to me. After the story, I answered a few questions. The truth was, the children took the news far better than I did. I told them that I now needed their help. Maddy's mom would be here in the near future to pick up her things and I was afraid that I would forget something. We needed to clean out her desk, empty her locker, and gather her name labels, which were in at least a dozen places around our classroom. It was incredible advice to give them a job to do. Somehow, this simple task helped us all.

We put all Maddy's things inside a beautiful big box I had purchased. The box stayed in our room for some time after. It was comforting seeing that box; somehow, having it there was like part of Maddy was still with us.

The book *Lifetimes* was so beautifully written that I purchased many copies to give away. It inspired me to write, and because I was so comforted through the book, I called my poem "Lifetimes."

Lifetimes

There's a time we get to spend on earth
With our family and our friends
This time seems like forever
But then this lifetime ends
Somehow time that seems so long
Is over in an instant
I'm sure when we go home at last
This lifetime will seem distant
God gives us all a purpose
To accomplish here on earth
That was established in the heavens
Long before our birth
Lifetimes are all planned
With a beginning and an end
But that is only life on earth
For then we will ascend
Into the everlasting life
God promised through His Son
And now for your loved one
A new life's just begun

That year I lost three people at my school in a short time. Yvonne, friend and teacher aide, had a relapse of cancer after eleven years. Then, a parent of one of my students lost his fight with leukemia. I knew him as a parent, yes, but he was also an incredible pastor of a large church in our city. I was confused! What was God thinking?

I don't know why God would allow Maddy in my class to be so sick and lose the fight for her life. I don't know why my friend Yvonne's cancer returned in a terminal way after eleven years, or why leukemia took Pastor Rick out of a successful ministry.

What I do know, though, is that who God is doesn't depend on my understanding of Him. In our pain, we tend to forget what God is capable of, and that He has the wisdom to use His power for what is best for us.

All three people were close to death at the same time, so the waiting time was excruciating. In my pain, I asked God to give me a prayer poem that I could pray. I wanted it to help me and yet glorify Him.

My Offering

Heavenly Father, I come to You now
Allow me to feel Your comfort somehow
Restore in me Your faith and Your hope
For I am finding it hard to cope
I can't get my head around Your way
But in my heart You remind me to pray
Lord, You're so big, so holy, so true
All love and truth is found in You
So I give You my heart, my worries, my cares
For You are faithful to answer my prayers
I will wait on the solid rock I am standing
For my hope lies not on my understanding
But on the almighty power and grace
You demonstrated when You died in my place
And if You decide to take my friends home
Like all of us, Lord, they are really Your own

For who am I to tell YOU what to do?
For the past and the future is all found in You
I accept your decision, for You know what's best
Perfect love drives out fear and will help me find rest
So my heart, my soul, my mind I bring
As an offering to You, my Creator, my King

Losing a loved one, especially unexpectedly, is devastating. My mother-in-law was experiencing some stomach trouble, and since she was about to go on a trip, she decided to go to the hospital to get the problem solved before she left. The problem turned out to be pancreatic cancer, and the trip she took was not the one she was expecting.

I was so glad that our pastor, and friend, led the memorial. One of his gifts was being able to make God real to people as they mourned the loss of a loved one. At one service I attended, he said that our physical death was a comma, not a period. It is hard to get our heads around everlasting life, but my guess is that the time we spend on earth is only a small part of our life's sentence. This has always stayed with me.

The first year you lose someone you love is the worst. It is a painful year of firsts; the first birthday without them, the first Christmas without them. My in-laws had been married for over fifty years, so of course this was extremely difficult for my father-in-law. On the first anniversary of her passing, I wrote the following poem for him.

Forever

Today you've gone through all the worst
Today you've gone through every "first"
And though you always think about her
You've had to somehow live without her
As you persevere through the pain
Until you reunite again

God continues to give grace
Until you leave this earthly place
And live eternal life together
With the one you'll love forever

Being part of a church community can be an enormous source of strength. One of our own was diagnosed with cancer and things were not looking good. Our congregation gathered to pray for her. I knew Sandra, but not well. Our husbands played on the same baseball team and I knew her from various church functions. I was surprised and honored that God would speak to me with the poem I wrote during the time we had gathered to pray for Sandra. She was very close to many there and my heart broke not only for Sandra but also for those who were praying for her.

From the Inside Out

Dear Lord, I ask for healing
In my discouraged friends
I pray You'll show them favor
And a love that never ends
Reveal to them Your glory
And the power of salvation
And how it all applies
To their present situation
You say You'll answer prayers
That line up with Your will
And I believe that's true
Though Sandra's body's hurting still
When answers to our prayers
Don't seem to be expedient
You give us strength and hope and ask
For us to be obedient
One thing I know without a doubt
Is when we do our part
You may not heal the body

But You always heal the heart
I pray You'll hear the prayers
From Your saints as we cry out
As we ask You for the healing
From Sandra's inside out

The cool thing I remember about Sandra is that she loved to dance. Being raised in the Catholic Church, although we sang and played guitars and other instruments during the singing, I don't recall anyone ever dancing as a form of worship.

Dancing to express yourself was not new to me, however. I was in marching dance bands from the eighth through twelfth grades. Being a baton twirler required perfecting baton routines and choreographing dance steps to the music we played. I loved it. Even though the music was different, I could relate to the joy Sandra felt as she danced during special events at our church. I could feel a God-given gift flow out of her while dancing in church, just like I felt something special flow out of me on the football field years earlier. Even though I didn't know Sandra well, I felt something in common with her.

It was noted at her memorial that she was probably dancing with the angels. As you can guess, I had to write.

Dancing with the Angels

As a loving community
We come to You in unity
There's sadness in the celebration
Mixed with joy and anticipation
Of what eternal life will be
When at last we are set free
We trust that You will help us find
Comfort for us left behind
It's not about us but about what You've done
Eternal life through the death of Your Son
Help us to hear Your spiritual voice

As we try to accept Your choice
We place Sandra in Your loving care
Together with her family, we lift up in prayer
Lord, most of all, we ask for Your peace
As we come to celebrate Sandra's release
She can dance with the angels, with life You provide
May Your will be done, and Your name glorified!

One of my fellow teachers, whom I very much admired, had a son who died in a car accident as a young adult. I didn't know where she stood regarding God or prayer and I didn't want to appear all churchy and religious, but I did want to offer comfort. I was on our school's Sunshine Committee, and my part was to write out the card on behalf of our staff.

At times like this, you often hear, "Our thoughts and prayers are with you." I wanted to expand that a bit. And, of course, it rhymed.

Say a Prayer

Take a moment, say a prayer
Shed a tear because you care
Tears can often cleanse the soul
Rebuild the broken back to whole
It doesn't matter your belief
May this prayer bring some relief

"Lord,
Give our friends Your loving touch
For they need You now so much
Even though this isn't fair
Please show them You're always there
May they find their strength in You
And for us all, who love them too
Amen"

Years ago, I had injured my back at school while picking up a little boy so he could reach the chalkboard. When I was home recovering, I started getting a strange shaking in my legs. It would last anywhere from a few minutes to sometimes half an hour. It didn't hurt, but it was hard to teach with, and since it seemed connected to my back injury, I was off work and going to physiotherapy. I brought it to my doctor's attention, but he was baffled. So I had the elders at the church pray for me.

It was during this prayer time that Gil, one of the elders, felt he had a word from God for me. He said the doctors were not going to figure this out. That word gave me faith that God heard our prayers. However, I wasn't quite sure what to do about my condition without involving doctors.

In the meantime, I grew closer to God, since I wasn't teaching and I had more time to spend with Him. I prayed for answers. My back was getting better and I was eager to get back into my classroom. I felt God answered my prayers because I was able to see two specialists in record time. (The wobbling legs recording I sent them probably helped, since this did look very strange.)

The more doctors I saw, though, the more discouraged I became. They had no explanation for what was wrong with me. Without a real medical reason for wobbly legs, most of the causes came down to either a strange virus or, maybe, it was all in my head. Because I pressured them into trying to fix me, I ended up on some strange drugs that gave me other weird symptoms.

After one of my follow-up appointments, I came home extremely discouraged. The neurologist had basically said that there was nothing wrong with me and he noticed that I was not the happy person he had seen six weeks before. I was devastated they couldn't fix me and came home and prayed in desperation.

I heard, in an almost audible voice, "What do you believe to be truth?" In my spirit, I replied, "You, Lord, You are truth." Then I heard, "Then why didn't you believe Me when I told you the doctors were not going to figure this out?" I was so humbled!

Until then, I couldn't even write, as the battle raged in my mind, although I felt God was asking me to keep trying. Shortly after, I had a breakthrough. I got up and wrote this before I had my regular quiet time with God.

The Battle

Let not my will but Yours be done
For this is how the battle's won
My spirit is willing to do what is right
But oh in my flesh there is such a fight

The war that goes on in the depths of my mind
Repentance and rest I wrestle to find
I reach for the armor that You provide
And call for Your Spirit to walk by my side

Oh Lord, how I struggle to gain understanding
But that is not what Your will is demanding
You've given me faith and hope through Your Son
And that is where the battle is won!

That morning, I could not believe what I read in the devotional book I used at the time. The reading for the day was the account of Jesus praying in the Garden of Gethsemane before his arrest and death on the cross. He prayed so intensely that Luke 22:44 says, "And being in anguish, he prayed more earnestly, and his sweat was like drops of blood falling to the ground."

Meanwhile, he had asked his friends to pray for him and they fell asleep! But when the real crisis came, Jesus was full of courage and strength. I tend to think of prayer as being the preparation for the battle. But could it be that it is the battle itself?

Hebrews 12:1 says, ". . . let us run with perseverance the race marked out for us." That's what I learned from Sharon. Everything she did was done with perseverance and passion. One thing I admired about Sharon was her way of balancing her life. She had many interests and made sure she had time for each one. Sharon and I taught at the same school. She taught full bore from February to June. That left her seven months to pursue her many other interests.

I first met Sharon while skiing at Silver Star. On the chairlift, she told me she was going to school to be a teacher. I hadn't been teaching long, but assured her it was a rewarding profession. Little did I know that in the years to come, we would teach more together than ski together.

Sometime later, I was in a skiing accident and had surgery on my thumb. A large cast prevented me from writing. I didn't want to give up my class for six to eight weeks, so I asked for a teacher-on-call for the afternoons, to help out with the writing end of the job. I got the cream of the crop—my friend Sharon!

It's not often you teach with another teacher, but we were a great team. Sharon never did anything halfway. Our class presented a circus, complete with gymnasts, tightrope walkers, and clowns on stilts. We even shot a child out of a cannon (well, a garbage can—this was Sharon's idea)! I was excited when she got a teaching position at my school, Mission Hill. She had such a love for children and a simple way of turning first-graders into gardeners and scientists and butterfly specialists, not to mention readers and writers. I was always excited for her to tell me all about the children who would be moving from her class into my second-grade class.

Then the unimaginable happened. I had gone into the school to finish up some work over the weekend. She was preparing for a substitute teacher because she couldn't shake the cough she had. She and her husband had just come from seeing the doctor and she didn't look well. When I asked what the doctor had said, all she could say was that it didn't look good.

The unspoken words were unbearable to think about. Later the diagnosis was confirmed to be lung cancer. How could that be? She was one of the fittest people I knew. She ate a healthy diet, kept fit, and had a wonderful family. She was not only a friend but someone whom I admired deeply. This just didn't make sense. My sorrow came out in rhyme once again.

Waterfall of Tears

Sometimes I just get crying and it's hard to stop the flow
Of the many tears I cry, even though I know
That my God is the master and He always knows what's best
I need to do just what He asks, and let Him do the rest
There's so much more I'd like to do, so much I'd like to say
But as I wait to hear His will, instead God just says, "Pray"
I try to be obedient, and let Him do His part
But can't He see to lose my friend is ripping up my heart?
He reminds me of her qualities, and all that I have gleaned
From the friendship that we've shared, I'm glad He intervened
For I believe He chose her to be a friend of mine
And I will have to trust in His perfect plan's design
I won't give up praying, it's important to have hope
For that's how God gives strength, it's the only way to cope
I pray that God will act upon the pleading prayers He hears
And make a healing river from my waterfall of tears

Shortly after I heard of the diagnosis, I was crying and praying, and crying some more as I drove through town. In desperation, I asked God to give me a sign that everything was going to be okay. Then a rainbow instantly showed up and gave me so much hope.

Sharon's life exemplified God's love to the fullest. Faith and hope beamed from her being, about how she would beat this monster. Yet I couldn't help but think of the "what if." To my knowledge, she didn't attend any church and we had never discussed faith or religion. I wanted her to be ready . . . just in case.

I certainly didn't know what to say, or how to broach the subject. So, I asked God to give me a poem for her. It was 5:00 a.m. when I felt a gentle divine nudge to get up. I looked at the clock and my mind said, "Lord, even if it's a poem you want me to write, we have plenty of time, it's Sunday morning!" But by 5:30 I just had to get up. When I started to write, these words seemed to write themselves on the paper.

Jesus Your Friend

In your search for wellness
May you meet your closest friend
He was there at your conception
He'll be with you to the end
He loves you like a brother
Protects you like a dad
He shares your happy moments
He's with you when you're sad
He knows you on the inside
More than anybody can
He looks past your human weakness
For His Father had a plan
He sent Him as a baby
Told the world He would come
He was a good example
Of what we should become
But because we all fall short
And don't always get it right
Because we can't beat death
No matter how we fight
We have a friend and Savior
Who died for each of us
He humbly gave His life
Out of His deep love for us
Not only did He die
For all our human sin
But He was raised from death
To give us life within
This life is everlasting
It's a gift He gives for free
Only sometimes in our weakness

We are blind and we can't see
So He waits patiently
For the decision is our own
And when we learn to love Him
Then He can bring us home

After completing the poem, I realized that God was not only telling Sharon something, he was also assuring me that in her search, she would find Him. It was going to be all right, for Jesus himself said in Matthew 7:7, "Ask and it will be given to you; seek and you will find; knock and the door will be opened to you." Even though we never spoke about the poem, I knew she would find what she was looking for.

As the weeks went by, I tried to prepare myself for what was ahead. Sharon was so strong through this journey. I continued to receive tremendous gifts from her as she showed me how to have not only faith and hope but also strength and contentment in the worst possible situation. She was still sowing seeds into my heart.

So, what about the rainbow? I wondered about that too. I read that poem as part of what I shared about Sharon at her memorial. Afterwards, her father introduced himself to me. He thanked me because he had been praying for her salvation. He felt that what I shared was a confirmation that Sharon had found God before she left us. I'm thinking that the rainbow was a sign that even though her physical life was taken, her spiritual life was saved.

I will finish this chapter with what I learned from all of this. The amazing part is that I wrote this poem *before* any of the above happened.

He Will

He doesn't promise to make the pain go away
But He says that by your side He'll stay
He'll guide you, teach you, see you through
Because He cares so much for you
So quiet your spirit, your heart, your soul
He's waiting to comfort and console
And reveal the knowledge of His will
As you enter His presence so quiet and still
He'll speak to you in a still, small voice
But to listen to Him must be your choice
So close your eyes, Let Him gently fill
You with His Spirit
Because He will

For the Family

When a baby is born, it is a big event in the immediate family, and also in the extended family and their circle of friends. In some churches, babies are christened or baptized as infants. In our church, we don't baptize babies; we dedicate them. The parents are promising to do their best to raise their baby according to God's will and seek His direction. (This is the *parents'* decision and the decision to follow Christ and be baptized is left up to the child when he or she is ready.) The ceremony is much like a baptism, and the whole church stands in support and prayer for this new little one.

This next poem was for such a babe. Unfortunately, I wrote it long ago and did not write down any details. I can't even remember who it was for. What I do remember is the excitement I had as a parent who shared a belief in the importance of raising your children to know Christ. Interestingly enough, I did record the scriptures that inspired my ideas (Psalm 51:10; Psalm 19:10; Ephesians 6:7; Philippians 4:12–13; Ephesians 2:10; Philippians 2:12).

Dedication Poem

As this small child is offered
Into Your loving care
We recognize her qualities

Are quite unique and rare
For You have planned for her
A path that's all her own
It was established in the heavens
Yet still not fully known
May You create in her
A purity of heart
Showing those around her
That she is Your work of art
May she grow to find Your word
More precious than pure gold
And fill her with Your joy
As her little life unfolds
Instill in her a soul
That follows after Thee
Help her develop a servant's heart
To serve wholeheartedly
May she learn to be content
In every situation
Developing self esteem
And the realization
She was created for Your pleasure
And for her parents' too
May she reflect Your love
And the character of You
Give her parents the tools
To build a strong foundation
And work with You to raise her
As she works out her salvation

I was adopted as a baby. There was never a dark day when my parents sat me down and told me the big secret because it was never hidden. I always knew I was adopted. My parents would always say, "These are our three beautiful adopted children."

I had a congenital cataract in my right eye. The adoption agency told my parents to think about this because there were going to be many doctor visits, various surgeries (this was 1957), and a chance of blindness. From the legal point of view, there was a choice to be made. But from my mom and dad's point of view, there was nothing to think over at all. They chose me immediately with no reservations.

When I grew up, I realized that God loves us all with a perfect kind of love, and it is His choice that we all will follow Him and feel His love. I then felt that I was special because I was chosen twice.

Some good friends of ours did respite care for a young toddler who was being raised by her grandparents. It became evident that a point would come where the grandparents would be too old to look after this young one. Our friends fell in love with her and were eventually able to adopt her into their family.

Chosen One

We gather today in celebration
Over the glorious confirmation
That you now share the Batchelor name
Though not where you originally came
But you were chosen, for God had a plan
And God upheld you with His hand
In spite of the obstacles you went through
He knew the perfect home for you
He chose a family with love overflowing
To pray for you as you are growing
You can be sure you are never alone
For they have adopted you as their own
And as they teach you about God and His Son
May you be proud to tell everyone
God's love for you will indeed suffice
For you, Monisha, were chosen twice!

We also had the pleasure of another adoption. This adoption was also very different from the one I personally experienced. I mentioned earlier Ray and Mary Anne, our pastor and wife who had been to Africa and were involved in housing and schooling children whose parents had been killed in the Gatumba massacre in 2004. One little boy obviously left footprints in their heart and eventually became their son. Not only did I admire them for the missionary work they did in Africa but I admired their commitment to raising a child who was young enough to be their grandchild.

Even though we find it hard to make sense out of war and tragedy, God is able to turn even the ugliest situations into good. In this case, this little boy, Boss David, experienced the blessing of two sets of parents who loved him as well as being introduced to his Heavenly Father. There is no doubt that God has a special plan for this young lad.

Triple Blessing

You have a special purpose
Mr. David Boss
God is always with you
No matter what your loss
He wants to bless you richly
But not in earthly ways
He'll bless you on the inside
With qualities that stay
Your blessing isn't yours to keep
Although it has great worth
For you were born to share it
During your short time on earth
God chose two sets of parents
To bless you with their love
Besides the Father God
Who parents from above
Pouring out His love for you
Through your parents He's expressing
The purpose that He has for you
With a triple blessing!

You give birth or adopt a child, and the joy and the love you feel are above your wildest expectations. And even though you do your very best to raise them and make decisions on their behalf, sometimes they want to fly away from the nest before you think they are ready, or before you are ready to let them. So, you put them in God's hands. This was the case with our oldest daughter. So of course I prayed.

Placed In Your Care

Lord
Take care of our daughter
Now that she's all grown
We place her in Your loving care
As she goes out on her own
We've done our best to raise her
Still it's hard to let her go
It's time to watch
The seeds we've planted
Take root and start to grow
Bless her as she travels
On the road You've planned for her
Help her know that of our love
She always can be sure
We pray that as she meets her world
She will know just what her part is
But wherever she decides to go
Home is where her heart is

Our son went through a bit of a rebellious stage. I prayed for him a lot! I remember asking him why he could not learn from the mistakes of others. His response? He wanted to make all the mistakes himself. What does a mother do with that? Knowing that the consequences of some mistakes can shape the rest of your life so negatively, hearing this was like a knife in my heart. However, he also said that he wanted to be a Christian one day, but just not right now. I was hoping that

that was God's way of giving me hope, and I fed my hopelessness with this rhyming prayer.

A Mother's Heart

Dear son,
There are things you ought to know
But are so hard to say
So many things I'd like to change
If I could have my way
The path that God's laid out for you
And sculptured from above
May be very hard right now
But was prepared with love
I see the pain you're going through
And I go through it too
Many times I find myself
Praying hard for you
I want to make it better
Like I did when you were young
My mouth wants to yell things out
But God says bite my tongue
The Father knows my aching heart
He feels the aching too
He waits for all His children
The way He waits for you
He wants to be the first one
You turn to every day
He knows what the future holds
And wants to lead the way
So if and when you're willing
We can go to God together
Because even when you're hurting
He loves you more than ever
So enter in His presence
For I know His peace is there
For God reveals His truth
When we go to Him in prayer

This prayer didn't bring me a transformed son instantly, but God met me supernaturally on several occasions so I could help him get back on track.

One evening, I was just going to bed when I had this overwhelming feeling that I should pray protection over our son. This happened when designated drivers were just starting to be used. Eric had gone out with friends to a local pub and had assured us he had a designated driver who would get him home safely. I trusted him and felt confident of his safety, so this thought that entered my mind seemed strange. I ignored it at first, but it was persistent. I prayed a prayer of protection over Eric and went to sleep easily.

The next morning, Eric had a horrifying story to tell. Yes, he had been drinking, but as he met his friend who was supposed to stay sober, his friend told him he couldn't take him home after all. He drove off, leaving Eric to pay for a taxi home. He was not impressed.

The next morning, we found out that this friend had indeed been drinking and had had a car accident after leaving our son stranded. The passenger side of the car was all crushed in.

Maybe these trying times don't happen in all families. But if they happen in yours, I can assure you that you are not alone.

I had heard that the enemy can blind you, especially during the teen years. It's as if he puts a veil in front of your eyes so that you don't see what God would like you to see. I felt this was happening to our daughter. My pattern of prayer was my go-to solution.

The Wandering One

Father, please show compassion
Forgive all the sins of her youth
We ask that You puncture a hole
In the veil that shadows Your truth
Let it unravel the threads that are binding
Your child from seeing Your light
Please give her Your revelation
Provide her with courage to fight
Be with her as she wanders
Away from Your loving hand
She has walked out from under Your blessing
For reasons we don't understand
We know that You are all knowing
And we know You won't cross her will
But please link Your angels around her
And reveal Your love to her still
Be with her, protect her, and guide her
Make fertile Your seeds deep inside her
She has left what she knows
Not knowing what she sows
Yet we know You are always beside her

I wanted so much to express how the relationship we have with our Heavenly Father is similar to the relationship we have with our own parents. You see, everything you have read in this chapter so far was written from a parent's perspective. I want to end this chapter with a story from a daughter's perspective.

After I finished writing this chapter, I was reading in the book of Kings. I was saddened by the fact that even though some of the kings in the Old Testament were totally committed to God, their sons did such evil in God's sight. I was wondering if maybe they didn't take enough time with their own children (must be hard having so many!) to teach them about God.

God calls us all to be like children. When you are an infant, you totally depend on your parents; you have total trust, and soak in everything they teach you. That's how God the Father wants His children (us) to be. Then we get a bit older and we want to try things our own way, but we stumble and fall. Our Father helps us up and is there to comfort us. By the time we get into our teens, we are embarrassed to be around our parents, and we want to grow up all at once. We think we can do it all by ourselves. We go through hard (and sometimes sinful) times before we learn for ourselves God's great love for us. But if our parents, or someone else, planted seeds in our lives, we are so joyful when we recognize that we have the choice to become one of God's precious children. That's what this poem is about.

As Christians, we can always go back to the Father's lap and be like little children. That's where He likes us to be.

A Father's Daughter

When I was an infant in my father's arms
He kept me safe with love and protected me from harm
And as I tried to walk, my little feet would stumble
But he held my hand and kept me out of trouble

As I grew a little older, I liked having my own way
I would argue with my siblings and thought this was okay
Then I could hear my father coming, and I knew right away
That I was in the wrong and there'd be a price to pay

Slowly, as the years went by, I became very self-reliant
As with many young adults, I grew a bit defiant
I'm sure he felt abandoned and at times held back his tears
And gave me to his Father to protect me through those years

I couldn't see the Father's hand that was protecting me
It carried me to hell and back but always was unseen
Until my eyes were opened to the darkness and the light
And I could feel that I was precious in my Father's sight

Even though my dad's now gone the greatest gift he gave me
He introduced me to *his* Father
The King who came to save me!

It is important to me to mention that even though this poem seems to be about my father only, I think of my mother and father as one. So this is really about both my parents.

As We Grow

"We don't need more to be thankful for –
We just need to be more thankful."

~ Carlos Castaneda

As a teacher, for years I collected sayings to put at the end of my weekly newsletter to the parents of the students in my class. The above quote is one of them.

I often taught split classes. At the end of my career, I taught the class as one group and adapted for all the levels. However, when I first started teaching, the trend was to teach with more of a split in instruction. One year I taught a little boy who was a first-grader in my first- and second-grade split class. Often I would have a different set of instructions for each grade. This little boy was really struggling until we realized he was listening to the wrong set of instructions (a really good reason for changing my teaching style!).

Like that little boy, there are times when we let ourselves concentrate on the wrong things. Often I feel that God is right there beside us when we are feeling all befuddled and sorry for ourselves, saying, "Open your eyes a little wider; you are concentrating on the wrong thing and you are totally missing the blessing I have for you!"

God doesn't only say he won't leave us or forsake us. He also says, in Romans 8:28, "And we know that in all things God works for the good of those who love him." Also, 1 Thessalonians 5:16–18 says, "Rejoice always, pray continually, give thanks in all circumstances;

for this is God's will for you in Christ Jesus." In essence, we have much to be thankful for, so open your eyes and ask God to reveal it to you.

This next poem reminds us not only that God is there for us and with us, but there is often a blessing as well, if we are patient and look for it with His help.

Blessing in the Burden

There's a blessing in the burden
If you strive to seek God's face
For whatever you are going through
He's sure to give you grace
He said He'd never leave you
And His word is always true
He loves you as a Father and
He even weeps for you
And this is why He's sure to send
Encouragement your way
He longs to let you know
That He hears you when you pray
If you let Him give His comfort
And lay your burden at His feet
He'll provide a blessing
To make the sour sweet

There are times, for all of us, when life throws us a curve ball that we don't expect. When my husband and I were young, with small children, we hung out with three other couples. We played baseball on the same team, we played volleyball together, went camping, had murder mystery parties, and so on. We were tight. So, of course it came as a shock when one couple split up. My heart was broken for my friends. I knew my girlfriend was searching for spiritual help at that time, so I told her I would pray for her every day. This was a prayer poem I prayed as if I were her. Reading it now, I can see how this could apply to many messy situations we find ourselves in.

Teach Me

Lord, take away the bitterness that's deep within my heart
Give me eyes to see the way to make a brand new start
Bring to mind the good things I remember from the past
And redirect my attitude to what you want to last
Let me feel Your Spirit as You walk right by my side
Fill my heart with joy that only You provide
Help me feel Your presence for I know it's only You
That will bring me through this desert that I feel I'm going through
Fill me with Your word and fill my heart with song
Keep my eyes on You so I see how to be strong
Help me not to worry, rearrange my point of view
Teach me how to hope and put my faith in You

Most of us go through situations that seem out of our control. I read somewhere that most people we meet up with in a day are going through something difficult, just went through something difficult, or are heading into something difficult. If there are so many people going through hard times, it stands to reason that they may be open to having somebody pray for them. Even if they think there is only a chance something good will come out of it, they feel they have nothing to lose. I have noticed that most people will accept prayer for their situation, even if only as a last resort.

Wanting to believe that God loves you unconditionally is the first step to letting it happen. Hence this poem.

Can I Pray For You?

God is loving, God is kind
And you are always on His mind
His never-ending love for you
Is waiting there to comfort you

Can I pray for you?

He's slow to anger, rich in love
He sent Jesus from above
To teach you how He wants you to be
And how to fight the enemy

Can I pray for you?

He's waiting for you to invite Him in
So that He can forgive your sin
For He loves you through and through
And He wants you to love Him too

Can I pray for you?

Christmas and New Year's Day come every year. I record the highlights of our family's activities and include them in my Christmas letter. For me, it is also a time of looking back over the year, evaluating the past in order to improve the future. This could be making lifestyle changes like diet or exercise, goals for saving money, planning home improvements, or career goals. It can also be a time for finding a new spiritual direction.

The following poem is one of spiritual direction. I could tell that I had gotten into the habit of asking God why whenever I ran across troubled waters in my life. As the poem materialized, I realized that if I knew *why* Christ came, I didn't need to know the reason behind my troubles.

Why

One thing I've learned and I'm trying to apply
Is to have faith in God without asking Him why
Our God is so big we can't figure Him out
And that is a good thing, there is no doubt
So when trials come, don't face them alone
Release them to Him who sits on the throne
He can and will handle any circumstance
Our problem is we don't give Him the chance
When Joseph and Mary welcomed a Son
It was prophesied that He'd be the one
To reunite us with Our Father God
To some, today, that concept seems odd
But what an example that Son was to be
A living example for you and for me
So as we celebrate His birth
Let's not forget why He came to this earth
He's spreading the word about salvation
He's gathering His flock for a Kingdom Celebration
Not just on Christmas, but all the year through
Your Savior has so much love for you!

Once I figured out that I was missing a personal relationship that included unconditional love in my life, I went searching for it. The love from my parents was close to this, but it wasn't it. I loved my husband more than I could say, but that wasn't it either. When I had my children, that was amazing, but something was still missing. When I realized that there was only one place to receive perfect love from, I *wanted* to put that source of love first in my life.

There is a scripture that talks about where your treasure is, your heart will be also. We can't be totally committed unless God is our treasure. But if, as Matthew 6:33 says, we seek first the Kingdom of God, everything will fall into place anyway. "But seek first his kingdom and his righteousness, and all these things will be given to you as well."

The ultimate metaphor is that we must be faithful just as in the bond of marriage. When we think of the marriage vows, "for rich or for poor, in sickness and in health, in good times and in bad times," it's easy to know that God cares this way for us. But in a marriage vow, both the bride and the groom say this vow. Can we be that committed to God? God *is* that committed to us and he is ready to teach us how to be that committed to Him.

In John 21:15–17, when Jesus kept asking Peter, "Do you love me?" He was really trying to drive His point home that it can't just be a whirlwind romance; Peter had to be committed.

It was this line of thinking that led me to write this poem.

Do You Love Me?

Do you love Me? Am I first?
Is it Me for whom you thirst?
Or have you put something else before Me?
I need your all, if you adore Me

Do you love Me? Am I number one?
Are you dedicated to My Son?
Or have you forgotten to make Me the center
And daily make time for My presence to enter?

Do you love Me? I have to be sure
Will it be Me for whom you endure?
Where is your treasure? For your heart will be
With anything that you have put before Me

Look to Me, let My kingdom come
Lay down your burdens, let My will be done
I will take you out of your slavery to sin
And will give you grace and mercy within

Do you love Me? I'm jealous, you see
I want nothing to come between you and Me
Come into My arms and stand by My side
For I am your husband and you are my bride

Knowing you were created with such love and with such commitment is very comforting. But *why* were we created? Oswald Chambers answered this question in two different wordings in the early 1900s: "The whole human race was created to glorify God and enjoy Him forever." And, even more simply, "I am created for God. He made me."[1]

If somebody asked me why I had children, my answer would be that I wanted to love them and enjoy their love in return. My husband and I created them out of our love for each other in order to love them and receive their love.

I can see certain family traits that were like gifts passed down to our children. I can see my curls in my grandson. I can see my love for rhyming in both my daughters' writing. My son picked up the love of playing guitar from my husband. Some of these gifts came from our genetics and some from our passions.

I believe that God also passes down gifts to His children to be used for the unique purpose He has for us. Sometimes we must learn to use these gifts in the right way. My oldest daughter was a very driven and motivated teen and young adult. She knew what she wanted and how to get it. As a teen, she caused a bit of confrontation in our home, but as an adult, she is a very organized nurse and mother.

Just like the good things my husband and I passed down to our children, they also received the challenging parts of our characters as well. But if we were born with no challenges to overcome, how could we experience the joy of overcoming adversity, and the friendships that helped us overcome them? And here's a thought. How about seeking help from the one who was without sin and is capable of

---

[1]   Chambers, Oswald. *My Utmost for His Highest.* Barbour Publishing, 1935.

perfect unconditional love? These were the thoughts that went into rhyme this time.

Gifts

Sometimes we take for granted
Or just don't realize
We are unique and special
In our Father's eyes
Our character was crafted
So carefully by His hand
He gave us faults and virtues
That we strive to understand
We struggle through mistakes we make
And try to go it alone
But our Father's always there
So we're never on our own
The weaknesses we carry
Give opportunity
To seek our Father's guidance
With closer unity
We enjoy our giftings when
They make us feel good
But we can use them wrongly
Not doing what we should
Our lifetime is a training ground
To use what God has given us
Until we learn to listen and
Be taught from Him within us
Our gifts were not designed
For our fortune and our fame
But to enjoy His presence
As we glorify His name

If we were created by God out of His love for us, and so that He could enjoy the love we give Him in return, how does this all work when we can't even see Him? I often wondered why Jesus went through all that pain and sacrifice of being nailed to a cross on our behalf, rising from the dead to show us we could have eternal life with Him, and then ascending into heaven where we couldn't see him anymore.

I enjoy reading books where people have died for a short time but are brought back to life. One of the consistencies in these stories is the mode of communication they experience. There is a spiritual way of communicating that we can't really get our minds around but from all accounts seems fast, efficient, and effective. In our human way of communicating, this is impossible. Maybe Jesus had to go so that His Spirit could communicate with all of us spiritually and not be confined to the human body.

So, how do we use this spiritual way of communicating right here, right now? We must train our ears and our hearts to listen. That is what this poem is about.

The Holy Spirit

God is with us through His Spirit
He speaks and teaches; can you hear it?
Let not your sin get in the way
For then His voice seems far away
Opening your heart to His salvation
Keeps a two-way communication
Spending time with God each day
Reading His word and learning to pray
Will give the Holy Spirit permission
To work through you and fulfill the mission
That God has chosen just for you
He knows what you are able to do
God's Spirit confirms just who you are
While making you His shining star!

Knowing that the Holy Spirit is there and giving Him permission to work in your life is a wonderful realization, but it doesn't mean it is always easy. There are so many things that try to claim our attention all day. Besides the challenges in the work place, the demands of a young family, and life maintenance, there are also physical limitations in our body that demand our immediate attention. Once we've discovered that quiet, happy place with the Holy Spirit, we want to be there, but there are often many things in life that distract us. I have found, though, that if I pray for it, it happens.

No Distractions!

Lord, in my spirit there is such an attraction
Yet in my body there's so much distraction
Deep within my bones there cries
A spirit struggling to arise
Above the physical limitations
To meet my Father's expectations
Breathe Your breath into my soul
Without You I can't be whole
Quiet my mind so I can see
Everything You have for me

As I said, there are many distractions in this world and there never seems to be enough time for what we *think* we need to do. Ahhh, but maybe there is . . .

I knew Pastor Rick as a parent of one of my students. He pastored a large church in our city and was well respected and loved. I enjoyed the chats we had from time to time. I could tell he put his heart into his work and I felt that, much like me, his brain didn't have an off button.

One day, I ran into him in the hallway after school. He mentioned that he was very busy and was finding it hard to get everything done. I related well to that! However, I always admired him for his calmness and the time he always had for his family. I said I would keep him in prayer. I thought about him as I drove home that day and thought about this "time" thing. I had been praying a lot for myself in that area lately. I really wanted to write a poem about it but of course . . . I didn't have time!

I started cooking supper and wrote down some thoughts as they came to me. Wow . . . there was this poem. That evening, I had to pick up a few things from Wal-Mart and was pulled into the picture frame section. One particular frame jumped out at me immediately. I bought one for him and one for me. We both ended up with this poem in our offices at home.

Eighteen days later, I spoke to him again and he had just learned that his leukemia had returned. I promised to pray for him and his family as I had before. He said he would take my poem with him to the hospital in Vancouver. I was honored, but thought that was strange, since he wouldn't have the stress of his job there. Again, I found myself praying for him on my way home. The poem came to mind and I realized that I had written it in the context of a day, but maybe it was also meant for a lifetime. I went straight to the poem when I got home and read it with different eyes. No wonder he wanted to take it with him.

I never saw him again, but he blessed me with the same poem I wrote to bless him. I look forward to seeing him again, in God's perfect timing. I hope this poem blesses you in whatever space of time you need it.

Time

God has perfect timing
And He tries to teach us too
That everything He asks of us
There's time enough to do
And yet we still get flustered
At our life's hectic pace
But He says to stop and

Keep your eyes fixed on His face
For He will give you rest
In your heart you know it's true
He will always give you time to do
What He has asked of you
So before the stress you're carrying
Is more than you can bear
It's time to seek your Father's face
And go to Him in prayer
For timing is His specialty
You won't be disappointed
If you stay within the plan
Your Savior has anointed

In Romans 7:19, Paul writes: "For I do not do the good I want to do, but the evil I do not want to do—this I keep on doing."

Sometimes, it seems that even though we know what we should be doing, we seem to make the same mistakes over and over. It's like our heads are in a fog and we just don't see situations clearly. It takes away our ability to reason, and can manifest itself in many ways, such as drug addictions, depression, alcoholism, or even overindulging in things more socially acceptable like shopping, eating, or gossiping. Any kind of struggle may overtake you to the point that you feel you can't be expected to make a clear decision. But you must!

Whatever your struggle, no matter how foggy your brain has gotten, you must remember that God is the lamp unto your feet. You may not be able to see the whole journey, but you can see a few feet in front of you, with the light of God. He will show you what you need for the first few steps, so take them.

Often when I used to go to school in the morning, the sky in downtown Vernon was like pea soup, but by the time I got to the top of Mission Hill, I was in beautiful sunshine. Even if it's an uphill foggy battle, God is still there.

No matter how foggy your brain is, you can still call on Jesus' name. He may not instantly produce a cloudless sky, but He will be the lamp unto your feet so you can find your way. God can do some miraculous things if we totally depend on Him and take those first steps. Don't miss what God has for you because the weather is gloomy. That is often when He shows His greatest power.

Get Out of the Fog

Lord, be the lamp unto my life
My heart is lost in so much strife
Burn off the fog that clouds my soul
Let Your wisdom make me whole

The morning fog has closed me in
Wrapped me in guilt from all my sin
But then I let my Savior in
His death has burned up all my sin

I look ahead, my journey's long
I think of all that I've done wrong
But step by step I move along
For Jesus is my victory song

The sun is starting to shine through
Oh, I see a hint of blue!
Father God You've made me new
Because of Jesus, I see You!

So, how do you get out of the fog? Take time alone with your Father in prayer so that He can talk to you. That's what Jesus did. As the Son of Man He needed to do this, and by being such a good example, He was teaching us to do the same.

Foggy thinking is not the only thing that gets in the way of learning to communicate with our Heavenly Father through His Spirit. Pride is a *big* stumbling block. Sometimes it is just plain hard to be humble and admit that we are wrong. Oh, we may apologize to show how humble we are, and then add a "but . . ." to justify our behavior. This suits us just fine because we have shown we are humble and at the same time we have justified what we have done wrong. Our wall of pride is really tall here. After all, don't we look so, so good because our action is justified and we *still* said we were sorry!

But if we are really honest with ourselves, we know that God sees right through this, even if the person we have offended doesn't. He wants to break down this wall around our hearts and help us deal with what is behind our clever disguise. If you are not finding peace in your heart, maybe your wall of pride is higher than you think.

Wall of Pride

As I go through daily struggles
Your presence seems so far
I see things as I am
Instead of as they are
My mind is in a turmoil
So I put on my disguise
But You see deep inside me
With Your penetrating eyes
I'm lost deep inside myself
Even though I know
You wait with perfect patience
With the answers to my woes
Lord, help me take the baggage
That I'm carrying to the cross
Restore in me Your peacefulness
That somehow I have lost
I seem to have this wall
Protecting me inside
With a sign that says "Keep Out!"
Let me hang on to my pride
You have so much to give me
Help me to believe it
Prepare me on the inside
Make me anxious to receive it

Break down the wall around my heart
Show me what to do
Help me focus not on me
But fix my eyes on You

We are all imperfect human beings involved in complex relationships. Sounds like a recipe for disaster. That is why forgiveness is the center of Christianity. That is why we teach the Golden Rule and try to teach our children to see their situation from the other person's point of view.

When I had to deal with two children involved in a conflict on the playground during my teaching years, I would often ask, "How do you think your friend is feeling right now?" Or, "When I ask your buddy here to tell me what happened, what will he say?" It was a real mind-shift to teach this because kids really just wanted me to punish the other for what they did wrong. Once each child owned their behavior we could move on to forgiveness and making things right again.

When you can't forgive someone, you end up letting bitterness rob you of the joy God intended for you. I can't even imagine how many times He has forgiven me and shown me mercy when I didn't even admit my wrong-doing. And He calls us to do the same . . . with His help. God is the perfect person to help us because He loves us all the same. Yes, it is a tall order, but if we see those who hurt us as God sees them, it becomes easier.

Forgiveness

Bitterness within the soul
Prevents us from becoming whole
Sometimes we must let things go
Forgiving those who hurt us so
We need to learn a life of love
Through the Holy Spirit above

Who shows us mercy undeserved
For God's mercy's unreserved
He forgives us even though
We don't deserve it and we know
That we can never get it right
No matter how we try and fight
The war of spirit and of flesh
But God's Spirit will refresh
Forgive us, Lord, our sinful deeds
As we forgive and intercede
For those who trespass against us
In our heart we know we must
Because we know whatever we do
To the least of our brothers
. . . We do unto You

That all sounds so good in a perfect world, like in a movie where everything all works out in the end. But in our day-to-day life, the movie keeps going and it may not feel like the happy ending is just around the corner. So how can we make this work in real life?

One way is changing how we see the problem in front of us. My husband used to be a ski instructor and ski coach. He was a darn good one too, because he was very patient teaching me!

In my early years of skiing, I would try and keep up with my husband and our friends who were all good skiers. There was one run that scared me spitless because it was steep and had trees on it. Not only that but you had to hike up a hill to get to it! Of course, this run was the group's favorite, so I would go along and try to look like I was having fun. However, inside I was afraid that I would not be able to turn fast enough to avoid hitting a tree or falling into a tree well. And believe me, I had videos playing in my head that confirmed these fears!

But one day, my husband, in all his wisdom, tried a new approach with me. Instead of reminding me of all the turning techniques he had taught me in the past, he made it really simple. He just told me not to look at the trees, but to concentrate on the spaces between the trees. Bingo!

The Skier

A skier loves the mountains
The winter and the trees
And there are many lessons
To be learned from all of these
Skiers don't mind hiking
Up the mountain for a run
Their muscles may be burning but
Fresh tracks are always fun
Skiers dress for weather
Because good skiers know
Often colder temperatures
Bring the powder snow
And most important learn the lesson
Of how a skier sees
He keeps his eye upon the spaces
Not upon the trees

So when circumstances in life seem like mountains too high to hike, or your heart has grown cold toward those around you, or you tend to see obstacles instead of open highways, learn the lessons from the skier.

Our life is like a book and there are tests along the way. Looking back, some chapters are so exciting we would like to reread them over and over. In my book of life, I like to reread riding a two-wheel bike for the first time, twirling my baton in front of our marching band, getting married to the love of my life, giving birth to our three children, teaching school, and being a grandma! But there are also chapters I don't wish to relive by reading them again. We all have such chapters in our book of life. Wouldn't it be wonderful if we could predict the last chapter and the ending of our book of life? Well, actually, we can. That is what this next poem is about.

Chapters

There are chapters in our life
We live through day to day
And if we let Him, God will guide us
Showing us the way
Some chapters we live happily
And finish with a smile
Reliving happy memories from
The past once in a while
Other chapters we close tight
Too painful to revisit
Not willing to remember all
The sorrow they exhibit
We live on through the book of life
As we advance in age
And sometimes it gets harder
For us to turn the page
Thinking of sweet memories
The ones we wish could last
We know we must move forward
Not stuck within the past
Looking at the footprints that
We've left back in the sand
Two sets reminds us of the times
We took our Father's hand
Other chapters leave one set
And we remember He
Carried us when we were weak
Or too sick or sad to see
All things work together
For good for those who love
Almighty God our Father
Who's helping from above
Sometimes those painful chapters

Take on a different light
Because we learned to listen to
The voice that made things right
Knowing that your book of life
Will be in print forever
And you will read it side by side
You and God together
Think about the ending that
You would like to see
And together you and Jesus
Can make that ending be

If you get anything from this book, I hope it will be that you are able to have a unique and personal relationship with God the Father, through his Son, Jesus, by way of the Holy Spirit. Experiencing such unconditional love from the creator of love in its purest form was so amazing for me that I just had to share it with others.

I hope you are noticing that this is not *religion* but a *relationship*. If you have read this far, I am guessing you must be a little bit interested in having a relationship with God yourself. When you do, I think you will find that you don't need more things to be thankful for, because just having a personal relationship with God makes it easier to be more thankful. Knowing that God has a special plan for my life and that He is always there for me is something I am very grateful for. On the days I'm not feeling it, I acknowledge what I have learned to be true, and pray something like this:

You Are There

When I am lonely You are there
To comfort me through personal prayer
When I am weary You are with me
Reaching down from heaven to lift me
When I am smothered in my sin
You open Your arms and let me in

And when I am weary and troubled and weak
You give me the wisdom that I seek
When I am anxious You remind me
That You continue to work inside me
Then I enter Your courts with praise
And You show me how to follow Your ways
You tell me I can trust in You
And everything You say is true
You draw me near when I venture afar
So I want to be with You wherever You are
You say You have a plan for me
Open my eyes so that I can see
For You say there's so much more for me
Something wonderful in store for me
Please give me the faith in my heart to believe it
And help me give thanks and have joy to see it

For Those Who Intercede

"... not giving up meeting together, as some are in the habit of doing, but encouraging one another—and all the more as you see the Day approaching." Hebrews 10:25

Meeting together is so important because what one of us lacks, another has. We are all missing traits that God would love to teach us and we all have gifts that others can learn from by our example. Often we think too much about what we lack, especially when we see that trait in someone else.

I was pondering this as various women got up to share at a ladies' retreat morning. It just seemed that many of us had reservations about coming and felt inadequate. I found myself drawing puzzle pieces on a scrap of paper. One of the women at our table saw my pencil going and asked if I was writing a poem. "Hmmm, maybe I should," I thought as I started combining my thoughts with my doodles. The following poem incorporates the things we learned as we spent our morning together.

Puzzles

We all are puzzle pieces in the picture of God's plan
Sculptured in the Book of Life before the world began

Our faith is tested by our trials and yes there will be pain
But evil done against you does not have to leave its stain
For the Mighty One who made you is always there to guide you
Waiting for permission to do His work inside you
He has purposely placed people who have just what you need
And you can give to others what they're needing to succeed
Each puzzle piece is quite unique but there's a perfect fit
And God places those around us, for our benefit
The partial picture on my piece can feel like defeat
But when we're all together the picture is complete

The next poem was written a long time ago (in the 1990s). I
don't remember what we were discussing at this women's meeting
but, I'm guessing it was about serving. As a young mom, I remember
feeling that I was there to serve my family dinner, but often didn't
get to sit down and eat it myself. As a grandma, I now see that was
only a short time in my life. But it seemed like forever during those
busy years. Yes, we are to serve, but we are still invited to enjoy God's
banquet table. I remember feeling so moved by the speaker that when
there was a dinner break, I drove home to my computer and wrote
this poem. I decided to center the poem before I printed it and an
amazing thing happened. See the angel? I wonder what God was
telling us that day!

Women of the '90s

We are not ordinary in these last days
He's giving us wisdom to follow His ways
He's made us unique and willing to serve
And He's given us grace that we don't deserve
For in Him there's strength that we don't understand
New mercies every morning to fulfill His plan
We are so special in His eyes
And He wants us all to realize
That often we just "set" His table

But He's telling us that we are able
To enter into His banquet meal
He wants to feed us, He wants to heal
And show us the way He really sees us
As sharing the love and the power of Jesus
So come now and eat because He wants you to see
The anointing He's given, He's setting you free!

As I hope you can see, we all need each other. I believe that we were born to live in community with others. Sometimes we naturally help others and sometimes we intercede with God so He will help them. Intercession is praying to God for someone on their behalf.

As a teacher, there were certain students I was called to pray for a bit more. One year, I was on an education leave so I could take a year of classes. For one of my assignments, I had to work closely with one student for a time and record the results. I chose a little girl whom I had taught the year before. This was not only a good opportunity for me but it gave her one-on-one instruction in a school system that couldn't afford to do that. I was learning how important it is to know what a child knows so you can relate to that knowledge and add to it as slowly as they need you to. And I have always believed that they must know that you care.

What Is a Teacher?

I'm trying to reach her
Because I'm her teacher
My job is sharing
My patience and caring
I continue to look
For that meaningful hook
Connecting the past
To ideas that will last
I pray that she'll see

An example in me
Of a loving touch
That she needs so much
So what is the feature
That makes you a teacher?
To do your part
You must teach from the heart!

For most of my teaching career, I taught at what was thought of as an inner-city school. Some of the kids had severe behavior problems, and there were also kids in wheelchairs (because our school had no stairs) and kids who came with no English-language skills (because we had the district's English as a Second Language, or ESL, program). I absolutely loved this because it was like a slice of the whole world in one building.

Being a Christian, I felt responsible to teach them all about God's love for them. Of course, this meant living it, not speaking it. I always asked God to show me how to really love my class and do what was best for each group of children I taught. It seemed the more challenging the class, the more I fell in love with them, and it was hard to say goodbye at the end of the year.

One year, I was just plain tired. I wasn't feeling the usual love. So of course, I prayed for it. One day, I was standing in front of the class, and in the middle of a lesson, it was there! I was so in love with the kids that I stopped and told them, "I don't know how you did it, but I love you all so much!" That year, with the help of a very talented teaching assistant, every child got a card with my picture on it that said, "I am special. I am different from everyone else. And Mrs. Wadsworth loves me." This next poem helps explain what I was feeling at the end of the year when I sent them off to the next grade.

Shining Son

I have them, Lord, for such a short time

Through Your hands You put them in mine
I fertilize seeds that were already sown
And plant new seeds but they're not my own
They are given to me by my Father above
To scatter and sow and tend to with love
I do my best as I progress them
Thank You for the chance to bless them
I place them in Your loving care
Release them with a simple prayer
Be with them through their days of rain
Until Your Son shines through again

Praying for others was something I learned to do when I was by myself with God. This intercession thing was like asking God how to pray for someone, then He would tell me, and I would do it. So when my daughter and her doctor found a mass in her abdomen, of course I wanted to pray the best and most efficient way I could. Waiting through tests is the most excruciating time there ever is. The wait time was supposed to be six weeks for an ultrasound and maybe even longer for a CT scan. I was beside myself, and she was even worse because her nurse brain would not turn off.

I decided to try a different approach this time. I asked God to help pray not just *for* her but as if I *was* her. She is a very organized mom and nurse and likes to be in control and have all her ducks in a row. And so I prayed this poem.

Out of Control

Lord, I am desperate and in need of Your peace
I desperately need my faith to increase
I'm told to give this burden to You
But Lord, that is very hard to do
I usually have things under control
I'm strong for others, for that is my role
But this, Lord, this has gotten me good

I can't control it like I think I should
So I need Your help, please show me the way
Teach me how to listen and how to pray
For this is so big and I just can't cope
I need You to help me and not give up hope
I can only see what I feel this minute
In this situation, and where I stand in it
But Lord, You have a much wider view
There is nothing that is hidden from You
I know You suffered and You got through it
And You can show me just how to do it
Help me to leave this problem with You
You are bigger than me and You know what to do
For You, dear God, have the knowledge I lack
Help me give this to You and not take it back

Not only did God answer the "how to pray" request, but we were so grateful to learn that the mass was not cancerous, and the problem was able to be corrected with surgery. What a faithful God we have!

Psalm 141:8 says, "But my eyes are fixed on you, Sovereign LORD; in you I take refuge—do not give me over to death." Finding peace is hard when you are overwhelmed by life's problems or when you are just plain scared.

When I went skydiving with my family (and I was petrified!), I was introduced to Vern, the skydiving master who would take me tandem with him, and Bob, the camera man who would video it. As I went through the short training session, and I mean short, one thing Vern said stuck out in my mind: "You need to keep your eyes on Bob."

I realized right away that keeping focused on Bob was the key to giving me the faith I needed to overcome my fear and enjoy the experience. I followed that one instruction to the max and I had a blast! In fact, I was more scared watching the video afterwards!

Maybe there is a parallel lesson in this to keep our eyes fixed on Jesus.

The Eye of the Storm

God's peace prevails
In the eye of your storms
His Spirit enlightens
As His word informs
The wind of the world's
Hectic pace
Takes your eyes
From your Savior's face
So open the eyes
Of your heart and try
To always look Jesus
Right in the eye
For He will provide you
With all that you need
If only you follow
And let Him lead

I have been involved in a few prayer groups, but I often feel I hear God more clearly when I am praying by myself. Years ago, I was friends with our church's youth leader and he asked me to pray for the youth. As I was praying at home by myself, I wrote the following as if God was speaking directly to the young people of our church. It came quite quickly and in an interesting format.

My Dear Children

I have made you special, unique in who you are
I want to use your giftings in your home or out afar
I'll cradle you in weakness because I look ahead
And plan to use your failures to glorify instead

Your learning and your struggles draw you closer to My side
I want you to remember, in Me you can confide
Sometimes I'll say, "Have faith," don't try to understand
Lift your eyes to heaven, and take hold of My hand
For I will lead you through this, I will never go away
But I will wait for you to ask, "Please show me the way"
And after you've invited Me to light the way for you
I'll give you all you need to work your problem through
You see, I am a carpenter, I have so many tools
And I will let you use them but listen to My rules:

Humble yourself and seek My face
For this is how to receive My grace
"Be still and know that I am God"[2]
Then proceed, when I give the nod
I want to have a relationship with you
I want in on everything that you do

The next poem came immediately after the first. It was as if the Carpenter was not only giving our youth advice, but He was giving them His tools to apply it.

The Tool Box

When you find that you have far more than enough
His **saw** will cut off all the unwanted stuff
When His ways seem fuzzy in your youth
His **screwdriver** tightens up His truth
Enjoy His gifts but when using your talents
Use His **level** to keep things in balance
His **safety glasses** will keep you protected
As you do the job that He has selected
And in the morning after you sleep
His **hammer** will pound His word down deep

---

[2]   Psalm 46:10. He says, "Be still, and know that I am God; I will be exalted among the nations, I will be exalted in the earth."

Here are His tools, please use them with care
Take them around with you everywhere
His Spirit is with you, you'll never be the same
Now go build His Kingdom in Jesus' name!

I hope you understand that God loves you more than you know and that He wants to have conversations with you. We live in a fast-moving world, and sometimes we think we can say memorized microwave-type prayers and they will do the trick. There is no trick! God doesn't *need* your love and attention, but He wants it so much, He created you for it. But He leaves the choice to you. Otherwise you would be His robot, not His child.

Sometimes I hear His voice so clearly, it is almost audible. Here is a story that includes one of our conversations.

A Conversation with God

One night, I was driving home from work and noticed a jeep had recently gone into the ditch, hitting a telephone pole. As I passed the jeep, a young man had just gotten out. I stopped to offer some help. Before I could even say a word, the young man yelled, "Go away!" Stunned, I realized he wanted absolutely no help. I got back into my car, thinking that maybe my husband could help, since we lived very close by. As I got back in my car, the man yelled in a desperate voice, "Thank you!"

This reminded me of a recent conversation I had with God. One morning, I had been praying for someone who was addicted to drugs. Even though she wanted to get better, she couldn't. I had been praying for her for years and things always seemed to get worse instead of better. Kind of like the man who hit the telephone pole, she was thankful for my concern, but just couldn't follow through with the help that was offered.

This troubled me and I asked, "Lord, I have been praying for her for a long time. You have given her a free will to choose You or not, and it is possible that she may never choose You to be her Savior. I am discouraged. How do You feel when this happens?"

Then I heard, "Yes, I have given her a free will, and if she doesn't end up choosing me, I will be disappointed."

"But," I continued, "You know all things. You know the beginning and the end. You know if she is going to choose You in the end, or not. I feel so discouraged. You must see this a lot more than me. How do you handle it?"

His answer? "I will never leave her or forsake her. And neither should you. Don't ever give up. I don't. Keep on praying."

Six months later, I was driving home from school and was listening to the news. I was shocked to hear that the father of one of my students was missing. He was also the father of my daughter's good friend. He led a troubled life, but he was a very nice man. My heart knew this was not going to end well, but when we heard he had been murdered, I was devastated for his family. I needed to really intercede this time. God gave me this poem that I still pray today.

Prayer of Intercession

Father in Heaven, I ask Your protection
On those who have strayed in the wrong direction
They don't know they're lost and, Lord, they can't see
The person that You have planned them to be
They are very much blinded by their situation
And are being misled by false information
Lord, please be fruitful without them knowing
Until seeds within them have started growing
Let Your truth be rooted deep within
For You are able to see past sin
Cover them with a blanket of love

Supernatural mercy that comes from above
Place in their hearts a revelation
That deep inside they seek salvation
Please break through the tough facade
And show them that they need You, God
On their behalf I intercede
Until they know it's *You* they need.

Matthew 28:18–20 is commonly referred to as the Great Commission.

"Then Jesus came to them and said, 'All authority in heaven and on earth has been given to Me. Therefore go and make disciples of all nations, baptizing them in the name of the Father and of the Son and of the Holy Spirit, and teaching them to obey everything I have commanded you. And surely I am with you always, to the very end of the age.'"

Once we personally know God the Father, God the Son, and God the Holy Spirit, we are all called to do this. We are God's children if we accept the inheritance, we are promised by accepting His forgiveness, enjoying His presence, and living under His authority. We will want to do this because it is hard to keep quiet about such an amazing love. All mankind is like that puzzle I wrote about earlier. We all look different and are called to participate in this Great Commission in different ways.

Somehow, people mix up rules and ritual with relationship. When that scripture was written, Jesus was talking to people He knew, people He loved and who loved Him. But He was also talking to us. He wants us to love Him simply because we love Him, not because we are afraid of breaking the rules.

When you get to know Him, and you are ready, He will show you the special quality He has given to you to fulfill your part of the puzzle, your part in His Great Commission. I try to pray this next poem often to help me stay on track with my part.

Morning Prayer

Lord, today I offer my heart
So I'm full of You right from the start
I plan my day but please guide each minute
So I can recognize Your presence in it
Remind me to pray for my family and friends
So they receive life that never ends
Open my eyes to see those who You place
Into my path because they need Your grace
Teach me to use the gifts You have given me
So others will see You working within me
Help me to be like a shining star
That's an accurate reflection of who You are
Help me repent so I don't block Your joy
For that is the strength in which I employ
The anointing You've given me for my mission
Fulfilling my part in Your Great Commission

For Those Who Forgive

"Father, forgive them, for they do not know what they are doing." ~ Jesus
Luke 23:34

I truly believe that sometimes the people who hurt us the deepest don't even know it. They see the same situation from such a different point of view, and from where they stand, they are doing the right thing. Or maybe they feel so much suppressed pain in their own circumstances that the only way they know to feel better is to inflict pain on someone else. It is more of a learned survival technique.

A recovering drug addict told me, years after she had stolen from me, that when she was stealing, it was necessary, not personal. I could see she really expected me to understand this and she did not know how deeply I, along with many others, had been hurt by her betrayal. By the grace of God, I was able to forgive her. My forgiveness did not excuse what she had done, but it did free me from holding on to a grudge or trying to get even. Because I left the consequences of her actions up to God in His perfect timing, I was set free of the pain that imprisoned me. Sometimes we are able to see the natural consequences of the wrongs done to us, and sometimes we never do. In any case, it is our choice to be a slave to unforgiveness or be set free from it.

Imprisoned by Pain

I say I forgive, but really the fact is
Really forgiving takes tons of practice
You cannot rehearse the grudge in your head
But must ignore those thoughts instead
Remembering God has had mercy on you
Should help you be able to forgive others too
Sometimes those who hurt us the worst
Don't even know it, and it's us who are cursed
We desperately want them to feel our pain
So we plan how to do it again and again
Our unforgiveness makes us a slave
Negatively influencing the way we behave
And then it is us who are needing forgiveness
Since none of us are ever sinless
Without forgiveness you suffer in vain
And are left to be imprisoned by pain
But if you forgive the way they behave
You'll be set free and no longer a slave

This is easier said than done, especially when it comes to family. In 1 Corinthians 7:28 Paul says, ". . . But those who marry will face many troubles in this life . . ." He wasn't discouraging marriage and family, but he did hint that it was inevitable that it wouldn't be easy. There are times when someone close to us hurts us, and we just can't shake it no matter how hard we try. We try to rectify the situation, but nothing seems to work. The problem becomes like a hard mountain in the depths our soul. When we feel it is humanly impossible, we must call on the One who can make *anything* possible.

Moving Mountains

I know that You can move mountains
But can You move mountains in me?
My heart has hardened so solid

In the place where no one can see
The hurt I carry from others
Has grown too enormous to bury
And the pain I rehearse in my thoughts
Has grown too heavy to carry
I have allowed it to grow
And I find it hard to be kind
I've tried to withdraw my love
And it's justified in my mind
By doing this have I hurt them
The way that they have hurt me?
For surely, Lord, they deserve it
So why am I not feeling free?
Have I made a mountain inside me
Based on the things that have been?
Have I become so hardened
That I can't even let *You* in?
I need You to move this mountain of pain
Because now I can't even see
That there is really some goodness
In these people who have hurt me
I have tried to make things right
But my efforts have all been in vain
I've done everything I know
But still feel enormous pain
Maybe I've played a part
In this situation we're in
Help me to love them like You do
And let the healing begin
If I give You permission to help me
Maybe You can achieve it
I don't know how You will do it
But give me faith to believe it
I know that You love Your children
And want us all to be free
Help me accept Your love
So You can move mountains in me

Isaiah 55:8–9 says, "For my thoughts are not your thoughts, neither are your ways my ways,' declares the LORD. 'As the heavens are higher than the earth, so are my ways higher than your ways and my thoughts than your thoughts.'"

It is hard to forgive others and not hold a grudge when we are hurt by their actions. Sometimes I think we hold a grudge with God because of terrible circumstances that we feel we don't deserve. When something awful happens, it is human nature to assign blame. It gives us a place to direct our anger. When there is no human to blame, we direct our anger toward God. After all, isn't He the one who is supposed to be in charge?

The book of Job illustrates how we should, and should not, react to terrible things that happen in our lives. It also shows us that there is a lot going on behind the scenes of our lives that we have no knowledge of. Job lost his whole family, every bit of wealth he had, and was covered in painful sores all over his body. Even when others told him to curse God, Job still put his trust in his Creator.

Most of us will never be put to a test like this. But I know two families who were tested to the limit. The Brunelles had three boys about the same ages as our children. But Glenda had actually given birth four times by that point. Rene and Glenda had lost a baby to a condition where the infant's skull was not fully developed and the baby only survived a short time after birth. I can't imagine anything more heart-wrenching than to give birth to a beautiful baby and lose him a few months later. After having all boys, they finally had a beautiful daughter named Cherise. Sadly, this baby died shortly after birth as well. I was so devastated by this, but at the same time, I was so strengthened in my faith watching how the Brunelles handled it.

In another family, the mother would have a very healthy baby growing inside her . . . until it wasn't. For a reason we may never know, her babies would die in her womb right before she gave birth.

I believe some people go through horrific situations in order to teach us how to deal with our own. These couples taught me so much because they reminded me of the book of Job. What if there really is a hidden battle going on that we cannot see? Job went through years of pain and still trusted God, and his story was recorded for all of us to learn that our God is faithful.

Losing a baby whose life is cut short before or shortly after birth can be devastating. But as Job taught us, God is still in control, and He is able to turn all things, no matter how painful, into something good.

Hidden Battle

There is a hidden battle, a war we cannot see
But we can certainly feel our spiritual enemy
We fight for our children and the children that they bear
For born and unborn babies in the world everywhere
They do not have a voice and yet we all assume
That everything is well, inside the mother's womb
With every single heartbeat, life keeps pouring in
With no anticipation of a problem deep within
And though there's lots of prayer and strong loving support
The unimaginable happens and a young life is cut short
Lord, help us not to blame You as we navigate through pain
Help us realize, that our suffering's not in vain
All things work together for our good within Your plan
Even though it's difficult when we don't understand

In Psalm 25:7, David prays, "Do not remember the sins of my youth and my rebellious ways; according to your love remember me, for you, LORD, are good."

My Aunt Toni always said that you never know how well you raised your children until they turn forty. She was joking when she said this, but the real message was that it takes time to mature and become less self-centered. She felt that by the age of forty we will show the true person we were going to be, good or bad.

For many of us, by this age, or maybe before, we will look back at our rebellious years and be ashamed of some of our actions, wishing we could erase them from our book of life. We try on many characters until we find the one that suits us best. Hopefully we have good role models in those years who will stick by us and lovingly teach us which paths will lead to a productive life, and which paths will lead to destruction. We always have the choice to learn from the consequences of our actions or blame these consequences on others.

Many of us had, or have, people praying for us for protection and guidance. And whether we know it or not, or even want to know it or not, God is always there waiting for us to ask Him into our lives. He is there to forgive our sins and give us the strength to overcome the most inviting temptations. But we must ask. This next poem was written for a loved one as she struggled through her teens.

Practice Person

Youth is a rocky road, not knowing where to turn
So many things you must go through, so many lessons to learn
We try on different characters until we realize
Which one feels the best for it's the perfect size
It takes a while to find it, though, you'll try on others first
Some you'll wear awhile and become well-rehearsed
But they will not feel right because they will not true
They are not the character that God has planned for you
He gave you special gifts so you could hear His voice
But He won't make you listen, it will always be your choice
There will be consequences from actions that you take
These are valuable learning tools so learn from each mistake
But often we don't want to learn so we cover our actions with lies
We try to escape the inevitable but something inside of us dies
Our hearts get hardened inside when confronted with the truth
That's why David asked God not to remember the sins of his youth
The good news is that God gives strength and He is always there
He will walk beside you when you go to Him in prayer
God is ready to forgive, but always remember the fact is
The person that you will become is always the person you practice

Addiction kills. That is a fact. You can overcome it, but you must *really* want to more than anything else. And even then, it may be too late. When it happens in your own family, it is devastating. Addiction controls behaviors that are justified behind a wall of survival. This makes it so easy to judge and be overcome by unforgiveness and hopelessness. But if we make sure we seek forgiveness for the sin in our own lives, we will be better equipped to pray effectively for those we love. James 5:16 bears this out: "Therefore confess your sins to each other and pray for each other so that you may be healed. The prayer of a righteous person is powerful and effective."

Searching

Lord, my heart is heavy today
Carrying burdens that won't go away
I try interceding again and again
And hope in the end that addiction won't win
How can I judge? For I'm guilty too
Nobody's perfect compared to You
I want them to know Your love and Your peace
So Your strength and power can be released
It's one thing to reach for lifestyle goals
But even with You, addiction controls
Justification for self-centered pleasure
Running after a counterfeit treasure
I can't make them stop, for You gave them free choice
But, Lord, please convince them to follow Your voice
For You know Your children cannot be complete
Without our sinful nature being left at Your feet
The realization that we cannot hide
Behind our justified wall of pride
Forgiveness and freedom is found in Your face
And because of Your love we find mercy and grace
But we must acknowledge just how we are wrong
And ask for Your help so that we can be strong
Then we will find rest and the love that's behind it

But we must be searching if we're going to find it

Matthew 7:5 calls us to take a good look at ourselves: "You hypocrite, first take the plank out of your own eye, and then you will see clearly to remove the speck from your brother's eye."

Maybe if we turn the "forgiveness" around for a moment, we can remember when *we* really blew it. Once I was running late and waiting to merge onto a busy street. I looked both ways and then back again to the left and there was a break in the traffic, so I merged in. However, the car in front of me did not, and I rear ended them. I felt ashamed because it was totally my fault. We exchanged information and I knew that I would be paying for the damage. But the couple did not ask for any money. They showed mercy that I did not deserve. Years later, I read something that reminded me of that day. When somebody shows us such grace and mercy, it is like they represent the face of our Savior, who is the ultimate giver of grace. Feeling that grace from others makes it easier to give it yourself.

Face of Grace

Heavenly Father,
I know situations aren't always fair
But I also know that You're always there
Help me to be a giver of grace
So those who hurt me see You in my face

When playing pool, you need to get the balls into the pockets, but you also need to know where the white ball will end up after each shot. You not only have to make the right shot, you have to make it the right way, so you get another shot afterwards. So, *the way* you make the shot is equally as important as *making* the shot.

There are times when our hearts are in the right place and we do the right thing, but because *the way* we do the right thing is not quite right, we don't get the full benefit we expect. In hindsight, we would choose to do things another way.

Keeping in mind the good or bad consequences of the choices we have is one way of saving ourselves from needing to acknowledge our wrongdoing and needing to ask for forgiveness. Sometimes we know our hearts are in the right place, but we don't think through the effects of our actions quite enough. Here is a prayer I wrote when I felt I did the right thing, but not in the right way.

Leaving Shape

Lord, You know I am hurting
And I'm seeking Your direction
You know that in my heart
I had a good intention
But things didn't quite turn out
The way I thought they would
And I would do things differently if
There was a chance I could
Lord, please teach me patience
In my life situations
So the way I do Your will
Exhibits my intentions
Your will is so important
But we really can't escape
From the *way* we do Your will
For we are always "leaving shape"

It is often said that hindsight is bliss. If we could truly see the future consequences of our actions, it would be so much easier to make the right choice.

In the days that Jesus walked the earth, He was teaching things that seemed to go against the religious culture of His time. We have the benefit of reading not only the accounts of Jesus' teaching but the account of His death and resurrection from it. It seems so obvious now, all these years later. But back then, it must have taken perseverance and time to keep in touch with what was happening when Jesus was teaching.

When I decide not to take the time to learn about the life of Jesus and what that means in my own life, am I ignoring the chance I have to see what He wants to teach me? Would I have done the same in the times of Jesus? Could I have been one of those who crucified Him?

Today, we have the advantage of so much information at our fingertips. Because of this, it is easy to get caught up in spending time in the wrong areas. We get to prioritize what we learn and how we spend our time. We have the benefit of inviting the Spirit of Jesus to live inside us to help us do this. When we do, our understanding of Him keeps growing. However, if our true intention is not to make Him the center of our lives, His truths will be hidden to us, just as it was to those who crucified Him. Hindsight *is* bliss. Are we using it? These were the thoughts I had one Easter.

Hidden

We now know the end of the story
Jesus rose in His Father's glory
Prophesied from so long ago
And yet the people didn't know
They knew scripture better than we
And yet they were blind and could not see
The Son of God was there among them
But they rejected Him and hung Him
Is it so different here today?
Do we kill Him another way?
Do we study the truth in His word?
Do we act upon what we have heard?
Do we admit that we truly thirst?
Do we make time to put Him first?
It's true He no longer walks beside us

He made it easy by living inside us!
But because we are so busy
We start to question, really, is He?
God doesn't let us understand
If we don't intend to follow His plan
The truth is hidden from our eyes
Until we start to realize
That what was hidden for so long
Was really right there all along!
We put Him to death almost every day
By choosing not to follow His way
But if we seek our Savior's face
And ask forgiveness by His grace
We're raised from death caused by our sin
Because we let our Savior in!
No longer will this Easter be
Just a day in history
But the day He set me free
By dying on the cross for me

Asaph wrote in Psalm 73: 16–17, ". . . it troubled me deeply till I entered the sanctuary of God. . ."

How does this work? God says that He won't leave us or forsake us. So, we should be able to say with confidence, like the author of Hebrews 13:6, ". . . The Lord is my helper; I will not be afraid. What can mere mortals do to me?" We should be able to scrape up enough faith within our souls to know that God is with us and is ready to help us in our present circumstance, even if we aren't feeling it.

Human frailty is another thing that gets between God's words of assurance and our own words and thoughts. When we realize how feeble we are in facing difficulties, the difficulties become like giants, we become like grasshoppers, and God seems to be nonexistent. But remember God's assurance to us in Hebrews 13:5: "Never will I leave you, never will I forsake you."

I Will Not Leave You

When mortal man has let me down
Where does my hope come from?
When days seem dark and nights are long
When will my answer come?
My eyes can't see, my heart is blind
I strive for answers I can't find
My ears can't hear, my heart is deaf
I feel like I have nothing left
But then I hear from deep within
The One in me who's always been
When you feel like life will break you
"I will not leave you nor forsake you
I am with you wherever you go
To remind you of what you already know
As far as the East is from the West
I will forgive, in your unrest
By using the strength that I will provide
You can do anything with Me alongside
So do not be anxious, but with thanksgiving
Let me teach you about forgiving
Whatever may come, you can persevere it
By listening to My Holy Spirit"

Based on Heb 13:5, Matt 28:20, John 14:26, Psalms 103:12,
Phil 4:13, Phil 4:6, Luke 23:34, Hebrews 12:1

Because Jesus died and took all our sin with Him, we have the gift of His resurrection and eternal life with Him. Because He left His Spirit to dwell in us, we can always enter His sanctuary and find peace.

Addiction takes many forms: drugs, alcohol, smoking, food, shopping, money, clothing, exercising . . . the list is endless. We often care more about how other people see us than how God sees us. Whether it is holding a beer and a cigarette with our friends, or having brand-name clothes or the best and biggest home, if we care more about what others think than what God thinks, we are being deceived. None of these things are everlasting, and taken to the extreme, will have the absolute opposite effect. And God has so much more for us.

Much More

I know you strive for greater things
And all that being successful brings
Striving to achieve the best
Appears to be a lifelong quest
You want the best but forget about Me
And earthly wealth is all you can see
My child, if you only knew
That I have so much more for you!
Your hard work seemed to work in the past
But earthly wealth will never last
Faith and hope and peace and joy
Are things this earth cannot destroy
If they're accepted from above
Together with My Father's love
Then these gifts will last forever
But we must work on them together
I know you feel you'd like to explore it
But often you put too much before it
I can help you here and now
Even though you don't see how
Take the first step so I can see
That you are truly seeking Me
Once you've chosen to receive
You can trust I'll never leave
Seek My kingdom, seek My face
And everything else will fall into place
For that is how I operate
And that, you can't negotiate
That's what hope and trust are for
Then I can give you so much more

Forgiving ourselves and others can be hard. Seeing things from another's point of view can be hard. Not judging others and owning our own mistakes can be extremely difficult. God has a plan for our lives, and when we mess it up, He forgives us and is able to help us learn from our mistakes. But He can't do this without talking to us. And we can't hear Him without taking time to listen to Him. Just like a rebellious teenager, often we don't listen because we know what we are going to hear. We would rather find someone to tell us what we *want* to hear. However, when we decide that we truly want to learn to listen, God's Spirit will be there and help us listen to learn.

Listening

God is always speaking but we don't often hear
Maybe we don't listen because perhaps we fear
That we will hear Him tell us something we don't want to do
And we would rather listen to another point of view
But if we truly love our Lord and give Him due respect
Then we will want to please Him and do what is correct
Listening takes practice, patience, and our will
To hear that still, small voice that will ultimately fill
Our hearts with joy and peace so others will be drawn
To the love God has for them and they can pass it on
If we truly love Him, then we will "feed His sheep"
And promises like this are very hard to keep
But God will not forsake us, He will guide us all the way
As we learn to listen to His voice throughout each day

There is something inside all of us that knows there is a higher power of some sort. Whether it is a tiny seed from our Father in Heaven, or the breath of His Spirit, or a yearning for understanding the purpose of life, there is something. There is also something that fights this.

I read about an old Cherokee chief who wanted to teach his grandson about this. The boy had broken a tribal taboo and his grandpa wanted him to understand why he did it. The wise chief told him that it was like having two wolves inside us; one is good, the other is bad. And they both demand our obedience.

The little boy asked his grandfather which wolf wins. "The one we feed!" said the wise old chief.

To be self-absorbed in a pity party when you have been wronged is not God's plan for you. In essence, you are feeding the bad wolf. We need to use the power of God's Spirit inside us to guide our thinking away from pity-party thoughts. We need to starve the bad wolf and feed the good. With practice and patience and the power of the Holy Spirit, we can be victorious if we die to our own selfishness.

Die to Self

Please help me be forgiving for I know that is Your will
I really, really try but feel angry still
I know the answer's hidden but can be found in You
Help me guide my thinking so I can work this through
If I can think of You and Your unfailing grace
I can use Your power in order to replace
My feelings of unrest, and thoughts will turn to joy
Because it is Your voice my spirit will enjoy
The You in me will grow and be watered by Your Spirit
The me in me will die as I let my soul hear it
And You will be victorious, overcoming sin
Because I died to self, and let my Savior in

Hebrews 8:12 promises, "For I will forgive their wickedness and will remember their sins no more." It is amazing to realize that God not only forgives our sin but forgets that it ever happened. And we are called to do the same. This is no easy task. In fact, it may seem virtually impossible!

When it comes to forgiving someone, the important thing is to begin by voicing your forgiveness. When our children were growing up and they had squabbles, we required them to apologize and forgive each other. It was often obvious they did this even though they weren't feeling it. But this was the first step in teaching them how important it is to say you are sorry and be able to forgive those who wrong you.

As I was growing up, I often heard, "I will forgive, but I will never forget." When there is unforgiveness, there is that uncomfortable feeling between you and the other person. You may even still feel angry every time you remember. So, what do you do with your anger if you keep remembering?

I recently heard it said that forgiveness is not that you forget, but you forget the hurt or anger attached to it. This makes a lot of sense because it is also said that not forgiving would be like drinking poison and expecting the person who wronged you to die instead of you. Without forgiveness, *you* are the one who suffers, while it is quite possible the person who wronged you may not even know that they hurt you at all.

Getting rid of the anger and the hurt is the only way you will ever be able to forget. Thankfully, God has left us His Spirit to guide us through the stages of forgiveness. After all, if we expect God to forgive us, then we should be ready to forgive others in the same way.

Receiving forgiveness and giving it are tied together. We tend to want to blame and direct our anger at someone. God the Father is perfect in every way and He felt the same way. So Jesus took all the blame and all the anger on our behalf. What a gift of love! And when we are ready to believe it, we can receive it.

Ready to Receive

Lord, I think I'm ready, please remind me what I've heard
For now I know Your truth is written in Your word
You say we are the branches and You're the living vine
Speaking to us personally through Your word divine
When comforting Your friends the night before You died
You spoke of things to come, and that You'd be denied

They didn't understand just why You couldn't stay
They wanted to go with You but didn't know the way
You were going to the Father and they could go there too
But the only way to get there was going there through You
That's not an easy concept and even though we hear it
We just can't understand it unless we have Your Spirit
You were just one person, when in Your human form
But now through Your Holy Spirit You are able to transform
For anyone who searches and wishes to believe
Has access to Your love when we're ready to receive

Based on John 14:1-6; John 14:26; John 15:1-8

One final thought from Mark Twain:

"Forgiveness is the fragrance that the violet sheds on the heel that has crushed it."

Is your life leaving a fragrance of forgiveness?

For Those Who Are Baptized

Rules and rituals can only be fully realized if they are based on a foundation of revelation and relationship.

*M*aybe you have never gone to church because your parents didn't or you have never found a need for it. Maybe you feel church represents empty rituals and outdated rules. Or maybe you went to church as a child, but feel that it is something your parents needed but you are far too busy to fit that into your life. After all, what you get out of it certainly doesn't merit the time away from your busy life to make it worthwhile. Or maybe you feel that you probably should, but you say grace, call on God if you need His help on the big stuff, and even say the *Our Father* once in a while. You may think, "I'm a good person. I believe in God. He loves me and looks after me. Everything's all good."

The last few examples above used to be me. I grew up in a wonderful Catholic church. I did rituals, followed the rules (for the most part), and was even the youth representative on the parish council. I was a *good* Catholic.

When I went off to college, I was so busy having fun and studying that I had no time for going to church. Once in a while, I would feel a pang of guilt, but then I would sacrifice that precious hour of my time to alleviate it and I was all good for a month or two.

I fell in love, got married, moved from Michigan to British Columbia, and became a teacher. And I did this all without the help of God. Or so I thought.

Then we had our first baby. Oh, how I wanted to do everything right! Of course, my background told me that we needed to baptize our daughter. When I suggested this, my husband said, "Why do we need to do that?" I was a bit shocked at this. Didn't all babies get baptized? All I could come up with was, "Well, I don't think she will go to heaven if we don't baptize her." The truth was, I wasn't sure that was true, and if it wasn't, I didn't know why. I just thought I had to follow the rules, and that one was important! After all, God made her, and I believed He loved her. Would He not let her into heaven because we didn't sprinkle water on her head? All of a sudden, I felt a little panicked because I really wanted to do the right thing for this precious baby, but I had no idea what that was!

This started a heartfelt search for something that seemed to be missing, but I couldn't quite put my finger on it. Life went on. We had two more beautiful children, complete with all the busyness that comes with having three children in less than four years. But the question remained, "What happens if you don't get baptized?"

About this time, I had become friends with one of our neighbors. We were both pushing strollers down the street at the same time and our kids spent time playing together. We were both stay-at-home moms, and she even went to a Catholic church. I had convinced my husband to go on Christmas Eve a few times, and I started going on my own, but this church wasn't like my church back in Michigan. I was trying to go, but it wasn't doing it for me, whatever "it" was.

Lorraine told me she was starting a neighborhood Bible study for stay-at-home moms like us. Even though I thought it seemed a bit "religious," maybe I would find this whatever-it-is that was missing. Also around this time, another neighbor who I had become good friends with was engaged to be married to a Catholic man. She wanted to surprise him by becoming a Catholic before they got married. She was planning to go through the program to become a Catholic and asked me if I would sponsor her. I replied that of course

I would, but secretly, I wanted the answer to that baptism question and many more questions that had been bothering me. I knew what I had been taught and had lived according to the faith of my parents. But what about *my* faith? Did I even have any? If I believed stuff that was so important to me, why couldn't I explain it or defend it? So, I decided that maybe I wasn't really a Catholic at all and that I needed to learn about it as an adult. I asked Lorraine to come with me as my secret sponsor.

By now, my unbaptized babies were seven, five, and three and I still had so many questions! The weekly program I was attending to get my neighbor Cathy into the church was amazing. Since I had started reading parts of the Bible in our little study group, I had learned to talk to God better and I was even learning that I could hear Him speak to me. That was the most exciting part! The people who spoke at these weekly meetings seemed to have a relationship with God like I was beginning to have. I really enjoyed listening to them.

However, my husband wasn't really interested in being Catholic, and I couldn't figure out why God would get me all excited to go to this church if Rick was not going to be part of it. This was certainly a stumbling block for me.

Another problem was that this baptism thing was still a big issue. My oldest daughter was going into second grade, which meant that she would be learning about communion in her Sunday school class. I had very sentimental memories of my first communion and I hoped that I could provide the same type of experience for my own children. This was a big problem, though. Because my daughter was not baptized, I was told that she could go through the classes but she would not be able to receive communion with her classmates. This was stumbling block number two.

Yet another problem arose during our last session of the weekly program to become Catholic. I was excited for this because the topic was on Holy Orders. This was when a man became a priest in the Catholic Church. The speaker was a monsignor. He was higher than a priest but not a bishop. By this time, I had witnessed a few miracles, I was learning to hear God speak to me, and I was feeling an amazing love relationship forming between God and me. This man was high up in the Church, so I was expecting an amazing testimony of how God had called him to teach others about this love that I was experiencing.

After he spoke, he asked if there were any questions. With great expectation, I asked, "How did God tell you that He wanted you to become a priest?" His answer stunned me. He said, "I never sat down and had a conversation with God, but if I do, I will tell Him you said hi." I didn't know quite what to do with that. All I knew was I couldn't be part of this church that he led.

The next Sunday was Easter, when all the new Catholics would be able to receive communion for the first time. I attended out of respect for my friend Cathy, but could not go back.

But now what? I hadn't ever attended any other church. How do you choose one? My husband suggested that I go church shopping and find a good one. If I found one I liked, he would come check it out. I took my three young kids to different churches, but none of them seemed quite right. I was getting discouraged.

I decided to try asking God about this. To my amazement, an answer popped in my mind! He said, "Ask Lorraine where she is going." I thought maybe I was making this up, or hearing things that weren't there; but it kind of made sense. I had heard that she had been checking out some churches, but we hadn't discussed this. Then God added, "And if they have babysitting, you will know that is the right church for you."

Oh my, was I losing it? Was I really talking to God and was He really answering? Lorraine happened to phone me about something and my insides got all fluttery. I got up the courage to ask her if she had been attending another church lately. She said, "Yes, we have." I could hardly speak. So here came the million-dollar question. "Do they have babysitting?" I asked. "Oh yes, they have a wonderful nursery. We are going this Sunday. Would you like to come?"

As you may guess, this church has been my church home ever since. My husband checked it out and it eventually became his church home too.

And yes, I did get the baptism thing sorted out. In this church, new parents "dedicate" their babies. This means that they dedicate them to God and promise to raise them according to God's ways. They pray for their baby and ask God to reveal His very special plan for their child.

When the child, or adult, wants to commit to this love relationship with God, they ask to be baptized. It is kind of like the commitment in marriage. You want to spend the rest of your life with your spouse because you don't want to live without them. You may not always understand their point of view, but you promise to stick it out. The cool part is the other person in this baptism relationship is actually capable of fulfilling the vows. God is always faithful. He will always be patient with you, never forsake you, and will love you unconditionally.

I wanted to make this commitment so I decided to get baptized as an adult. At this point, my husband supported my choice to start going to church regularly and wanted our kids to learn about God, but wasn't ready to buy into this church stuff regularly himself yet. He had to work the day I got baptized and I was crushed. I don't think he realized what a *big* deal this was to me, or what a *big* deal it was, period. But it was a *big* deal and there was nothing that could ruin it for me. I was excited!

Full-immersion baptism was foreign to me, but I was told that the water represented death since you cannot survive under water. When you rise up from the water, you have a new life with Christ, and the old life you had without Him has died. Yes, symbolism, and yes, ritual, but something different happened that I can't explain. Before I went under the water, our pastor asked me if I wanted to ask Jesus to do something for me. (Many years later, he told me this was not the norm.) I didn't have to think about this at all. It was like God was reading my mind. I asked that Rick would come to love God too.

Eventually he did, and I was so excited I asked God for a poem to give him. This is what God gave me.

Baptism

Your baptism, oh what a wonderful day
Making the choice to follow God's way
You've made the decision to make God the center
In all that you do - His presence will enter
A public announcement to Satan and all
You've heard Jesus' voice and answered His call
May God be the source of joy in your days
And His presence reflected in all of your ways
It's now time to let His will be done
Using His strength when it seems you have none
Whatever path that Jesus will guide you
His abundant strength He will provide you
Search for His kingdom, search for His face
The rest of your life will fall into place
He knows your needs far better than you
And His love will be there in whatever you do
You've experienced the wonderful revelation
That God gives free the gift of salvation
He has forgiven again and again
He died and took with Him all of your sin
He was punished by death, He stood in your place
He rose to provide you with God-given grace
A God of judgment, love, power, and glory
May you find excitement in hearing His story
For the more that you get immersed in His word
The easier it'll be for His voice to be heard
As Jesus said many times before
Go now my child and sin no more [3]
From this day on you won't be the same
For now you live in Jesus' name!

It is a wonderful day when you decide that you truly want to live
and acknowledge that you are a child of God who strives to be just

---

[3] Paraphrased from John 8:11: "No one, sir," she said. "Then neither do I condemn
you," Jesus declared. "Go now and leave your life of sin."

like your Father. To do that, you must trust His authority and be committed to Him first. To feel confident to do this, you must get to know Him. The only way to do that is to spend time with Him. So many people don't understand that a loving, two-way relationship with the Almighty God can exist.

When you realize it, you can't believe that you missed it for so long. You finally acknowledge that all those little nigglings in the back of your mind were really the Holy Spirit trying to get your attention.

You may know that the word *salvation* comes from a Hebrew word meaning deliverance, rescue, welfare, to save. But what are we rescued, delivered, or saved from?

When I was a child, I would occasionally misbehave to the degree that my dad would give me a spanking. This didn't happen often so when it did, I really knew I had messed up. There was one time, however, when my misbehavior warranted a spanking and I didn't get one. Instead of feeling lucky not to get the punishment I deserved, I felt worse! Knowing I had disappointed my dad put an uncomfortable distance between us that was far more painful. How I wished he would just spank me and my debt would be paid! Then we could be close again.

When a drunk driver kills another person or a child molester goes on trial, we want them to pay for what they have done. But what about "less serious" wrongdoings? When we do wrong to *any* degree, we create a distance between us and our Father in heaven. Because He is so full of love and perfection, we can't measure up to that, no matter how hard we try. Whether we get the consequence that our actions deserve or not, there will always be that distance between us and God.

God could have made us perfect robots that loved Him, but He didn't. He gave us the *choice* to love Him. When He did that, He also knew we would mess up. But He had a backup plan. He sent Jesus, who had no sin, to be punished in our place once and for all. He even told us, in Isaiah 53:5–6, that this was going to happen: "But he was pierced for our transgressions, he was crushed for our iniquities; the punishment that brought us peace was on him, and by his wounds we are healed. We all, like sheep, have gone astray, each of us has turned to our own way; and the LORD has laid on him the iniquity of us all."

Then in the New Testament we hear the same message in John 3:16: "For God so loved the world that He gave His one and only Son, that whoever believes in Him should not perish but have eternal life."

We still may have to pay negative consequences for our poor choices here on earth. But because we are forgiven by our Heavenly Father, if we ask, we are saved from being separated from that perfect love I have been telling you about.

My godchild was having an extremely hard time as she went through high school. She had decided to be baptized and had asked me to come up with her. Before the baptism, all those being baptized went up to the front of the church with the person they had chosen to sponsor them. They told why they had decided to be baptized, and their sponsor had a chance to say a few words and pray for them. I was deeply honored.

Knowing that she didn't feel worthy of God's love because of the turbulent time she was going through, I asked God for a special poem that would express His power to cleanse her and feel His everlasting, unconditional love for her. I not only got the following, I was told to buy her the whitest, fluffiest towel I could find and wrap her in it when she came out of the water, which I did. Revelation 3:5 says, "The one who is victorious will, like them, be dressed in white. I will never blot out the name of that person from the book of life, but will acknowledge that name before my Father and his angels." This all came out in the following poem.

Clothed in White

God has prepared you for this day
He's been calling you to follow His way
Today He has asked you to be His bride
To walk down the aisle of life by His side
And you have accepted His invitation

To receive His free gift, the gift of salvation
He has clothed you in beautiful garments of white
For that is how you are in His sight
The stains of sin won't leave a trace
Because our Savior died in your place
Today as I watch you get baptized
I'm so excited you've realized
That Jesus will guide you by His Spirit
May you always open your heart to hear it
May you let Him guide you to do what is right
And always remember He's clothed you in white

If you decide to live your life with Christ, it doesn't mean that all will be easy because you have a miracle machine at your disposal. It just doesn't work that way. If you are married, you may have felt that you and your spouse would live happily ever after. Then you realized it can be hard work! It is a bit like that with baptism. Just like in a marriage, it is easy to go day to day with all of life's obligations and then realize you haven't spent quality time with your spouse all week!

My mother gave me some excellent advice before our first baby was born. She told me that it was easy to be consumed with the baby and all the chores that need to be done. When you get that feeling, *fight it* and spend time with your husband. Life does get very busy, but if you don't spend time with your husband, it is easy to grow apart.

It is the same with God. You need to *make* the time to spend with Him so your relationship stays close.

One of my close friends was going through a hard time. She knew about God and had even started getting her family to go to church. At this time, though, she still hadn't made that important time to spend with God each day. As I swam my laps in the pool, I prayed for her. She was a busy teacher with young children at home, just like me. I prayed, "Lord, she has so much on her plate right now. What can I tell her that will convince her to put You first?" As I swam to the wall and made a flip turn, His answer was so simple, "Tell her I am the plate."

Spending quiet time with God gives Him the opportunity to speak to you and help you make changes in your life to become more like Him. Sometimes we ignore those little feelings God gives us when He is trying to help us change a bad habit. When we ignore it enough, it gets easier not to carry the guilt that is supposed to help us make a needed change. Hence this prayer:

Changes

Lord, please give me eyes to see
What You would like to change in me
Help my thoughts to rearrange
And give me strength to make the change
For it's been part of me so long
I no longer see it's wrong
And I've bought into Satan's lie
That I can't change this sin of mine
But, Lord, I want to be set free
And feel Your healing deep in me
You are the potter, I'm the clay
So mold me like You, this I pray

It's hard to make the changes we know we need to make. We all have our own ways of coping with life's challenges and trying to find that "something" that is missing. Sometimes these strategies may even work . . . for a while. What do you do?

What Do You Do?

What do you do to make yourself whole
When your situation is out of control?
Maybe you drink or smoke or eat
Or shop to make you feel complete
Whatever you choose for self-medication
Does it improve your situation?

Have you noticed it can be like a curse
That's making your outlook on things even worse?
Then maybe it's time to try something new
Like looking for God, because He's crazy about you!
He's watched you stumble, tumble, and fall
He's been ready to help you but you didn't call
But He would like you to try something new
And show you that He has a plan for you
Try talking to Him a little each day
Pretty soon your heart will start seeing the way
Out of the prison your spirit is in
Because He will change you from within
A few minutes with Him to start off your day
Getting to know Him is definitely the way
To find forgiveness for your sin
And move you beyond this place you are in
For now is the perfect time to start
Build your faith and give Him your heart
Jesus will never give up on you
He waits patiently for you to pursue
The life with Him so He can be
With you through eternity
Choose Him now, don't waste a minute
Of living life with Jesus in it

I wrote this poem shortly after the family tragedy that I referred to at the beginning of this book. My oldest niece died after being hit by a car. She was addicted to drugs. No matter how hard she tried, she could not free herself from this bondage. No matter how hard or how many of us tried to help her, she was in and out of prison, she lost her home, and she lost custody of her two beautiful daughters.

In spite of all her poor choices, she called out for God to help her, but the addiction was just too strong to overcome. I believe God knew her heart and He never gave up on her.

He loved her not because she did enough good deeds, or because she had a good heart, or even because she was a very generous person.

He loved her with His perfect love because she was *His* daughter, in spite of her shortcomings. And He loves all of us in that same way. I'm sure God welcomed her with open arms into the gates of heaven, because He knew that the desire of her heart was to seek Him.

In Matthew 7:7 Jesus said, "Ask and it will be given to you; seek and you will find; knock and the door will be opened to you."

But what if . . .

What if she would have made this choice and followed the way God had chosen for her *before* she got into drugs? What if she would have known this passionate Jesus and learned the truth He teaches through the word of God? What if she would have learned how to listen to God's voice and use His strength instead of her own to overcome the problems in her life? What if she would have pursued a personal relationship with Him, and spent so much time with Him that she started acting like Him?

What if we all did?

We aren't capable of loving perfectly, but we are capable of receiving this perfect love by saying yes to God's call to get to know Him, by confessing that we have done wrong and need Him to forgive us, and by being blessed by His presence as He changes us from the inside out

So if you haven't already, make today the day that you

**Say yes
Confess
And be blessed**

About the Author

Margaret Wadsworth grew up in Milford, Michigan. After high school, she attended Alma College to pursue a career in teaching. She took a term abroad and met her husband, Rick, in Chamonix, France. In their forty years of marriage, they have lived in Vernon, British Columbia, Canada where they raised three children. They have been family foster parents, and lead a care group through their church. Margaret has always loved children and taught elementary school for twenty-five years. She enjoys writing, playing pickleball, golfing, swimming, camping, hiking, and being with her three children, their spouses, and her grandchildren.

Printed in the United States
By Bookmasters